SOUTH STREET ∿∿∿∿∿∿∿∿∿∿∿∿∿∿∿∿∿∿∿∿

New York's Seaport Museum

SOUTH STREET

New York's Seaport Museum

by William Bixby

DAVID McKAY COMPANY, INC., NEW YORK

OTHER MCKAY BOOKS BY
William Bixby

Forgotten Voyage of Charles Wilkes

Great Experimenters

Havoc: The Story of Natural Disasters

McMurdo, Antarctica

Race to the South Pole

Seawatchers

Skywatchers

Waves: Pathways of Energy

Of Animals and Men

Rebel Genius: The Life of Herman Melville

ᥡᥡᥡ SOUTH STREET

CONTENTS

PREFACE

South Street was once known around the world as "The Street of Ships." It was a scene of tall masts and of bowsprits that arched over a cobbled roadway, of grogshops and countinghouses, boatbuilders, sailmakers, and chandlers; and the reason for its being was the grand hulls that were shaped to battle storms far at sea—the vessels that rested between voyages on the city's doorstep.

Remembering dimly, in confused fashion, how men built New York by driving windships across wide oceans, we have come back in our time to rebuild South Street. We found our way here, in ignorance and faith, by varied paths. What we have discovered in working to get at the truth of the South Street story has resulted in a great new museum for the City—a living museum that will always be part of the fabric of city life.

And that is important. We need a place where people can see how New York grew and thrived and what it was really like along the way.

We think, as this book suggests, that the story of men's tall dreams and hard work in South Street is a deep and rewarding tale, not to be captured in pat answers, set lessons, or programmed rules. It is a tale that rings in the songs men sang, the evident pride they took in their work, and the beauty and strength of the ships themselves. These things were conceived in freedom and shaped by respect for the discipline that freedom demands.

As this book goes to press we are only a few years away from an important "birthday"—the nation's Bicentennial in 1976. While birthdays and anniversaries are perhaps an arbitrary way of marking our passage through time, they serve a real purpose if they summon us to think about that passage and what we have become as a result of our national experience.

Where are we going? What's it all about? These are challenging questions and we would be wise to try to find answers in our time. We can learn from the men of South Street—men who built New York and did so much to build America.

We can learn—if we will. The lessons are not easy and do not come packaged for convenient use. But they are profoundly rewarding. It is a rich inheritance the men of South Street have left us. You can enter upon it here, in this book, and you can step further into it by joining the museum and becoming one of the people who makes South Street live today. There is joy in the work—joy and a lesson. It is evident in the way these men held themselves, how they named their ships, the very tone of voice that reaches us across the epochal years.

As you enter into the South Street experience you will find injustice and hardship and all the ills of men; but you will hardly mistake, I think, the splendor of men's labors and the value of the cargo that we carry on our voyage through history.

PETER STANFORD
President
South Street Seaport Museum

March, 1972

INTRODUCTION

South Street Museum in its final form will be a large, multi-million dollar memorial to New York and the time when New York was the leading port and the leading city in the world.

Within a few blocks located amid the high-rise towers of Manhattan the entire history of the city's nineteenth century life can be found. And since the rise of New York was due entirely to trade and shipping, it is correct to say that ships are what the museum is all about. They are not dead, forgotten and preserved ships, but ships that live and sail and work just as they did over a hundred years ago in many cases.

Anyone studying the growth of the city and of the shipping industry on both the East and Hudson Rivers, cannot help but be struck by the fact that New York was first a port before anything else. The wealth due to this and its vigorous exploitation by merchants and traders and ship captains led to the city's becoming the financial capital of the United States and to the founding of great fortunes.

Any book that attempts to portray the history of a major port must define where the port begins and ends. And this is at first glance an easy question. One might say it ends at the Battery and is defined by the piers and slips along the East River. But the ships built and sailed from a port are part of its history, and so immediately the scope of the book is extended to include Europe, the Indies, South America, China—in short, the world.

And since trade produced the wealth that built New York City, the port is a part of the history of that city's growth. It involves the banks, Wall Street, Broadway, the mansions and the hovels, the tenements, the railroads—everything that is in the city.

What of the immigrants who came through the port? Many stayed and helped build it; others went on to the prairies of the west and settled such states as Minnesota, Wisconsin, and Illinois. So those distant states are somehow entangled in the story of South Street.

There is clearly no end to the limits of a great port. And since there is no end, any attempt to enclose such a story within the covers of any book or volumes of books must always be incomplete, as this one is. No single work and no series of works will tell you all you may want to know about South Street. The best way to satisfy your own curiosity about the port and its history is to seek answers to your questions at the Museum itself. Ships, shops, shipyards, tools, costumes, food, drink, architecture—whatever it may be, it is all there.

SOUTH STREET ⌇⌇⌇⌇⌇⌇⌇⌇⌇⌇⌇⌇⌇⌇⌇⌇⌇⌇⌇⌇⌇⌇⌇

New York's Seaport Museum

1

~~~~~~~~~~~~~~~~~~~~~~~

Heyday

LIKE GIANT stranded narwhals, the ships lay along South
Street. Their bowsprits, serene and immobile, reached over the
street itself. Masts, yards, and rigging made a cobweb of the sky.
The scene reached down river as far as the eye could see.

Beneath the bowsprits, on piers alongside the towering hulls,
men swarmed like ants. Draught horses hitched to large iron-
wheeled wagons clattered over the heavy planking. Shouts, calls,
and whistles mingled with the crash of casks rolling down from
ships' decks along slanting, swaying planks. Iron rims of wheels

rang and thundered on dock and cobblestone street. Sailors, bound for sea, moved unsteadily from grogshop doors to outward bound ships. They sang and swore, oblivious of shorebound mortals along the way.

Here and there, well-dressed gentlemen and ladies (with parasols) searched amid all the activity for their packet that provided a safe, expensive, exclusive cabin. Behind them small blacks staggered under their load of wine hampers, wardrobes, and luggage beyond counting. Blue-coated mates and skippers moved easily among the piles of cargo on the docks. They talked, but in ordinary tones—the tones of authority. Young men from the country, pink-cheeked and overfed, wandered uneasily along trying to find the bowsprit and the great hull that would take them to sea for the first time. They shipped as "boys," lowest of the lowlife in the forecastle. Here and there, across South Street men of unshaven, furtive countenances, leaning idly against the buildings and warehouses, watched, gauging cargoes, observing departures and arrivals, noting cargoes on the docks that might be left there overnight and so provide a bit of loot. Bewildered, tired, pale immigrants straggled hopelessly among the litter and people. Here, at last, was the land of the free: A boundless, indifferent uproar. A few blocks away, in quiet offices and counting rooms, merchants wearing clean linen and peering through gold-rimmed eyeglasses sat behind large desks calculating the quantity of cotton, wheat flour, or hides they would ship to Europe—and what return cargoes they might expect for their ships. In counting houses, clerks' pens scratched on, filling the otherwise quiet air with the noise of their writing.

All day, every day but Sunday, through summer heat to winter snow, the vast unending bustle and uproar went on. This was New York; the greatest port in America. It was South Street; the street of ships. The year: 1850.

The midpoint of the nineteenth century was also the midpoint

South Street in the heyday of New York port was a forest of masts and rigging, literally, "as far as the eye could see." *Courtesy South Street Seaport Museum.*

of a period of phenomenal growth for this largest of cities and ports. The years from 1840 to 1860 are unmatched in any other port's growth. Imports from all countries rose from about forty-five million dollars to 248 million; tonnage through the port increased more than 360 percent while exports rose by more than 400 percent. Trade was the most important business in the young booming city. Near the beginning of the period there were more than 400 commercial houses and over 900 commission houses in the city which focused almost entirely on the piers and slips of South Street. Over two-thirds of all imports to the United States came by way of South Street.

Bankers and merchants operating successfully in the boom climate established fortunes that created the families whose names today are synonymous with eastern wealth. Criminals and gangs

5

flourished too. The cry for law and order was heard then as now. There was poverty aplenty in the growing city. Beggars and paupers, sick, indigent immigrants, all thronged the streets of what we today call "lower Manhattan."

Growth

Before the close of the War of 1812, South Street, which is to say the entire Port of New York, was in a natural race with such other eastern ports as Boston, Philadelphia, and Baltimore for dominance. But shortly after the war's end, all other ports were hopelessly behind in the race.

There were many reasons for New York's outstripping all other ports. Not the least of them was its natural harbor and easy (save for Sandy Hook shoals) access from the open sea. The North River (Hudson) and East River flanked the rock-hard base of Manhattan Island with plenty of deep water space for ships to dock and load or unload cargo and passengers.

Another reason was the foresight and imagination of New York merchants and ship owners. In the early days a ship's sailing date and route were haphazard things at best. The demands of trade might take a ship on many a zigzag course from port to port in search of cargo, or for a buyer of one already on board. Once in port and unloaded, the wandering trading vessel might wait for weeks to find a cargo to yet another port. And while this might have been profitable to a merchant in his office on Pearl Street, it played havoc with a passenger who wished to go from New York, say, to Liverpool as rapidly as possible. The gypsy cruising of ships was not a passenger's idea of the best way to do it. Of course, he had no alternative until 1818.

Before 1818, the best service a passenger could get would be on a trading vessel that sailed between two given ports, New York and

Havre, for example. But the time of such a vessel's sailing was as irregular as that of any wandering ship. For regular trade needed a cargo, and cargo was not always available at any desired moment. Then, on January 5, 1818, the *James Monroe* of 424 tons set sail in a flurry of snow exactly on the advertised day of her sailing. It was no accident. The concept of regular sailing dates, of using a fleet of ships for passenger and cargo crossings of the Atlantic on a fixed schedule, and of advertising that schedule and sticking to it, marked the beginning of what was later to be called "liner" service. And, of course, that concept still exists today, as the great liners move regularly up and down the Hudson River from westside piers.

The *James Monroe* was one of four ships owned by a closeknit group of merchants, one of whom was Jeremiah Thompson. He had made his fortune by importing wool cloth from England and returning cotton grown in the southern states. He is credited with organizing the first liner service, marked in New York by the *James Monroe*'s January departure. Advertisements of the sailing schedule showed the fleet of four ships at the top of the column in the newspaper.

Within seven years from this time, there were sixteen of these "packets" sailing between New York and Savannah; four to Havre; ten to Charleston; four to New Orleans—plus many smaller vessels going on schedule to lesser ports.

Another reason for New York's preeminence was the trade established on the opening of the Erie Canal. This major link between the seacoast and the new western lands had been considered many years before anything actually was done—as far back as 1784. The idea was to connect Lake Erie with the Hudson River by a series of canals and locks. Merchants of South Street and many upstate businessmen saw the advantages and in 1811 New York State made attempts to interest other states and the Federal Government in

The *James Monroe*, first transatlantic "liner," began regular passenger service between New York and Liverpool in 1818. *Courtesy South Street Seaport Museum.*

the project. All that came of that was good wishes from the states and the statement from the Federal Government that such help would be unconstitutional!

So New York had to "go it alone." South Street merchants, accustomed to risks in the shipping trade and possessed of a keen sense of the future possibilities of any enterprise, were strong supporters of the Canal.

In 1817, a new Governor, DeWitt Clinton, pushed the project and bit by bit, the canal was built. As each section was completed it went into service. But not until 1825 was the entire canal put to use. For that memorable occasion, Governor Clinton, aboard the

Seneca Chief, a canal boat, set out from Buffalo, New York en route to South Street. All along the way crowds gathered to celebrate this Canal's debut. The date of departure from Buffalo was October 26, 1825. The *Seneca Chief* arrived at New York on November 4th. The boat rounded the Battery and sailed up the East River to the Navy Yard. Ships of all kinds crowded the rivers and the harbors to welcome the first boat from Lake Erie. With Navy officers aboard, the *Seneca Chief* sailed back down river, through the Narrows to the open sea. Surrounded by boats, waving flags, guns and whistles, the Governor emptied a wooden keg of fresh water from Lake Erie into the salt water of the Atlantic.

The Canal was a success from the start, commercially and politically. New towns grew on the banks of the Canal. Trade through South Street increased. Immigrants coming through New York had easy access to the rich farm lands of the west. And the Canal returned all of its cost through tolls collected along the way.

In addition to the natural advantages of New York as a harbor and the inland route for commerce provided by the Erie Canal, another less dramatic but equally important reason for New York's ascendancy lay in what is called the "Cotton Triangle." Astute merchants looking for profitable trade soon realized that southern cotton was in demand in England and Europe. They soon developed trade relations with southern planters, often extending credit to insure a cargo and, further, to provide a steady source of supply. Like Jeremiah Thompson, these merchants imported woolens from England as well as machinery and fashionable items for sale in the southern as well as northern states. Ships sailed to southern ports and picked up cotton. They then departed for England. On occasion rum from West Indian ports was added cargo for ships returning to New York. This vigorous three-way trading brought South Street to the fore and kept it there.

On the opening of the Erie Canal in 1825, New York was at the

Lights from a coffee shop on a winter night reveal the South Street population of homeless women and children, drunks, and sailors. Murder was common and life was cheap. *Courtesy New York Public Library.*

peak of its first surge of growth. During the first part of that year five hundred new merchant houses opened. Twenty-seven new banks were required to handle all the added business. In that year also more than 3000 new buildings went up and 1300 ships sailed into the East River to dock at South Street piers.

The small town atmosphere of an earlier New York had all but vanished by then. Plans to light the city by gas had been made long before but not until 1825 were they completed. The first house lighted by gas was at Number 7 Cherry Street. The famed Chatham Garden Theater helped usher in the gaslight era which was to

10

persist until Thomas Edison displaced it with electric lights in the closing years of the century.

As New York City grew on the business brought in by the thriving South Street merchants, its banks became the financial center of the United States, and when railroads began to crisscross the land, the bankers and other financiers took part until their power stretched all the way to the Pacific Coast.

Wall Street was a business street from 1817 onward and Broadway remained the central promenade and thoroughfare. But with all the growth, came growing pains. The city government was not equipped by its structure to serve the city well. Attempts to change it were frequent but often ineffective. This was to be expected in a city where the population growth outraced all expectation. In 1820 it was 123,000; forty years later it had mushroomed to over 800,000 and among these stalwart citizens, there were some interesting characters that could easily have sprung from the pages of a Dickens novel. In the modern sense of the word they were criminals.

Crime

As the city grew, the original streets lined with elegant houses of the wealthy merchant class deteriorated. The wealth moved "uptown" and the older houses fell into disrepair. The poor and the criminal took over.

Today, reports of crime rates in New York City lead any reader to the conclusion that criminal matters are going from bad to worse. People are afraid to walk the streets at night; burglary and mayhem are rapidly increasing and police and political figures are gloomy. Compared with crime in the heyday of New York's growth, however, today's crime picture resembles a spirited but essentially harmless sewing circle.

As early as 1825, gangs began to form in the lower echelons of the port's burgeoning society. One direct aid to their formation was what were known as green-grocer speakeasies. Licensed to sell liquor by the drink in addition to groceries and other necessities of life, these establishments provided a relatively private back room for drinking, scheming, and drinking by characters who did not want too many people to see them in a public saloon. Nor did some of them wish to be seen together.

One Rosanna Peers, proprietress of such a "grocery" on Center Street, deserves her place in the history of South Street. It was in her back drinking room that the first organized gang in New York was born: The Forty Thieves. (Then, as now, swaggering and romantic names were devised for gangs.) This irregular group of thieves and murderers met in Rosanna's place to plan crimes and they were all too often carried out.

Within a few years there were some sixteen hundred such "groceries" and a great increase in the number of gangs. Some, like the Forty Thieves, were bona fide professional criminal groups and there was no hint of amateurism in their efforts. Others were of the more boisterous and brawling variety: The Chichesters, Roach Guards, Plug Uglies, Shirt Tails and Dead Rabbits, to name a few.

A typical member of such a gang wore a sort of uniform and strode the streets terrorizing all "civilians" and members of other gangs. Members of the Shirt Tails walked around with their shirt tails out to signify membership. The Plug Uglies, on the other hand, wore large plug hats stuffed with cloth and bits of leather to turn the hats into helmets which protected them in a fight. All gang members wore heavy hobnailed boots or shoes and when a gang fight broke out—or just a two-man encounter—heaven had to help the one who first fell to the ground. It was legitimate technique to stamp an opponent into submission and frequently into an early grave. Eye-gouging, biting, stamping—it was all one long joyful fight as far as gang members were concerned.

12

Each gang, of course, had its district and "foreign" gang members entered the territory at their peril. But if, as sometimes happened, a distant gang threatened a riot, then adjacent gangs would make common cause for the duration of the crisis.

Many of the gangs, like the Bowery Boys, were also volunteer firefighters and they took great pride in their esprit and their fire wagon. Others, like the Forty Thieves merely dressed as firemen, the better to enter a burning building in search of loot.

The favorite activity of most gangs, however, was fomenting a riot and at this they were very adept. Almost anything would serve as a cause. As Abolitionists raised their voices, the answer was a riot. A depression with high unemployment would do but an event did not have to be serious to start a riot. The Astor Place riot, as the story has come down to us, was sparked by nothing more than an English actor and a politician who did not like him—or any other Englishman for that matter. The English actor was to perform Macbeth at the Astor Place Opera House and the politician was determined to break up the performance. At first, he only managed to delay it. But a few nights later, the audience entered the theater between lines of special police units who were on the scene to protect the Englishman. By this time the riot-happy gang, under the leadership of the politician, had inflamed the lesser citizenry by harping back to the War of 1812 and rousing the hatred of all things English—including the harmless actor. The fight started and the police soon found themselves in trouble. The militia was called out and they marched briskly to the scene. By this time the street was jammed and the Mayor was on the point of calling for artillery support when the militia managed to quell the disturbance. The result: twenty-two dead and forty wounded.

It was not uncommon at all for uptown respectable citizenry to hear or see a company of army troops parading to the downtown sections where sin and riot lurked. And sometimes these same citizens heard the rumble and clatter of artillery going to support the infantry in one or another struggle.

Police, in those days, consisted of marshals responsible for districts. The marshals hired nightwatchmen. But the watchmen were on duty only at night, and frequently they had a beat that required two hours to cover. Most of them also worked during the day, so they were scarcely alert during the dark hours. The marshals themselves were paid on a fee basis, so they encouraged a bumper crop of crimes themselves in order to increase their take-home pay. All in all it was not a good system. The watchmen wore no uniforms for many years and they were identifiable only by a metal star, made of copper—and hence the name Cop.

So complete was the control that gangs had over neighborhoods, that in moments of tension, police hesitated to pursue a suspect too closely. And daytime police never went singly into either the districts or into a saloon or brothel in search of a wanted man. They patrolled, not in pairs, but in groups of six and upon cornering a suspect in a particular saloon, police would lay siege to it for several days rather than risk entering the establishment.

The gangs, then as now, were not without their female admirers. The involved ladies, however, did more than admire from the sidelines. In fact on many occasions, they supported the idea that the female is deadlier than the male. As a melee broke out in one street or another, the women "stood by" on the outskirts of the boiling mass of humanity, additional ammunition in hand in the form of spare cudgels, knuckles, clubs, and firearms. Frequently they brought food to the exhausted strugglers since the riots on some occasions lasted two or three days. Many of the more vigorous ladies joined in at any opportunity.

In the early sixties the highpoint of the era was the Draft Riots of 1863. In this nearly all the gangs of the city joined with the avowed aim of literally destroying New York. And in this fracas

14

the women proved themselves more than equal to the men. They fell to work on captured police, Negroes, or soldiers. They sliced the prisoners with knives, gouged out eyes and ripped out tongues and when the bodies were sprayed with oil, they gleefully lighted the fires.

One gang, the Dead Rabbits, had the distinction of appealing to one of the more ferocious of the fighting ladies. She was known as Hell-Cat Maggie. Her name was apt. She had, according to reports, filed her teeth to points and she wore long artificial fingernails made of brass, honed to as delicate an edge as her teeth. Plunging with bloodcurdling shrieks into the fray she could literally rip a man to shreds in only a few seconds. Once the stunned and bleeding preserver of peace fell to the ground, he was through. For the men immediately stamped him to death.

Another famous lady in the mayhem department was Gallus Mag, so called because she wore men's suspenders to uphold her skirt into which she had stuffed a pistol and a billy club. Of English origin, and over six feet tall, Gallus Mag served as a bouncer for a saloon keeper named One-armed Charlie Monell. His establishment, the *Hole in the Wall* on Water Street, held the enviable distinction of being the worst dive in the city—and it was later closed by a resurgent police force when the score reached seven murders there in two months. Gallus Mag, and another lady, Kate Flannery, were the bouncers and Kate was obscured by Gallus Mag's creative method of ejecting customers. As a bouncer, Gallus Mag would knock some complaining customer unconscious, and then drag the offending person to the door by sinking her teeth into one of his ears. If the pain brought the person to a state of too-complaining consciousness, Gallus Mag would bite his ear off, carry it in triumph to the jar she kept behind the bar, and deposit the trophy among others, pickled and visible as the days and nights increased her haul. But Gallus Mag was not without heart. In moments of sentiment when an ejected customer came back later, she might return his ear with some such placating remark as "No hard feelings."

In a thousand other ways, the ladies proved their usefulness and loyalty. Many were willing to lend a hand in the total abolition of a respectable citizen careless enough to wander into the maze of streets near the docks. As he strolled by, followed closely by two men intent on thievery, the lady accomplice would empty a bucket of ashes from a second floor window on the citizen's head. The fellow, blinded and momentarily incapacitated, proved easy prey for the following men. The next day, all that remained of the incautious stroller was his naked body lying in the gutter. He had lost his money, his clothes, his life, and his dignity.

A typical establishment of that day attempted to cater to the tastes of its lusty clientele. The first floor consisted of a saloon, the second floor held prostitutes, while the third and fourth floors provided rooms for rent. Liquor although of a nearly fatal poisonous quality, was cheap. The cost was three cents a drink but in many saloons such pricing was maintained only by passing up the glass. The customer put down his three cents and was handed the end of a rubber hose attached to a whisky cask. The customer could swallow all he wanted if he didn't take another breath of air. When the gimlet-eyed bartender saw a customer take a breath, the supply of whisky was instantly shut off. Naturally under those circumstances, breath-holding ability was a prized possession. Yet even with the low-priced whisky, many a man found himself running out of funds. In some places, when a man was down to pocket money of a nickel, he was led in his fuddled state to what one emporium called "The Velvet Room." There he was allowed to drink himself unconscious and to remain in alcoholic slumber until he woke.

One of the more respectable trades among saloon owners and frequenters on Water Street was crimping. Delicately put, this was the business of supplying sailors for crew-short captains of the ships lying along South Street. The simplest method was to get any given person—sailor and non-sailor were treated identically—drunk. When the man passed out, he was robbed of any valuables he might possess, and for a fee, his limp body deposited in the forecastle of an outbound ship. When the drunk woke, his first impression frequently was of the gentle rolling of the ship's hull as waves of the open Atlantic were encountered. And it might then be "Goodbye Jack" for a long time since whalers, for example, often spent three or more years at sea.

In later years the government put a stop to the free enterprise of crimpers but only after a committee reported that the thriving business handled 15,000 sailors each year and netted in the neighborhood of two million dollars for the effort.

Scarcely any street or street corner today in the South Street area is without its moment of history. The men who made their mark in the "underworld" of the day were river pirates, crimps, pimps, thieves, and murderers on a scale that is scarcely credible.

There was George "Snatchum" Leese for example. By night he was a river pirate, stealing from ships docked along South Street or swinging on moorings in the East River. By day Snatchum was a bloodsucker. He attended bareknuckle fist fights and when one combatant began to bleed copiously. Snatchum sucked the wound dry. No less colorful was Jack the Rat who eked out a living biting heads off mice, for ten cents a head. A rat cost a quarter.

And Slobbery Jim. And Patsy the Barber. And also staid John Allen who ran a "dance hall" at 307 Water Street.

John Allen's place, stocked at its opening with twenty black-bodiced girls soon became known as an outstanding dive. John Allen himself was termed by journalists the Wickedest Man in New York City. For John Allen was a religious man. His three brothers were preachers and he himself had studied for the ministry. But at some point in his earlier life he must have said to himself "To hell with it." Still, old habits linger. His girls were supplied with Bibles in their small utilitarian rooms. Three days a week, John Allen brought all the girls, bartender, and waiters together for a sermon which he preached with fervor and conviction. As services do, his included hymn singing and reportedly the girls' favorite was the following somewhat ambiguous lyric:

> *There is rest for the weary,*
> *There is rest for you,*
> *On the other side of Jordan,*
> *In the sweet fields of Eden,*
> *Where the tree of life is blooming*
> *There is rest for you.*

On special evenings, Allen distributed New Testaments to all of the night's customers. In this strange hall, sin and religious fervor co-existed uneasily until the ministers from the respectable part of town launched an all-out campaign to reform the debauched and debauching Allen. There were so many legitimate preachers holding services in Allen's hall that his business fell off and eventually the preachers won. The dance hall was closed one August morning and a sign on the door read:

THIS DANCE HALL IS CLOSED
No gentlemen admitted unless accompanied by
their wives, who wish to employ Magdelenes as
servants.

Virtue had triumphed, even on Water Street.

Politics

The explosive growth of New York in the middle years of the nineteenth century caught the crude planners of that day by surprise. City government was nicely arranged for a small town village

18

but it could hardly cope with the behemoth that New York was becoming. Non-uniformed police, moonlighting as watchmen, could not protect the citizens; volunteer fire departments—dozens of them—could not save lives or property; and dug wells here and there throughout the city could not supply water. It did not take the city's ward leaders long to realize that the Mayor and city officials were largely helpless. There was, for example, no voter registration law, no adequate poll-watching and no police to enforce the generally agreed-upon idea that only live citizens should vote, and they only once.

Ward leaders soon enlisted the support of the gangs and through the cooperative efforts of politicians and gang members, the era of nearly complete political corruption in New York City was off to a rousing start.

One of the pioneers in corruption was a Captain Isaiah Rynders who became one of the most powerful Tammany bosses in the city. He owned the Sixth Ward; he had the allegiance of every major gang chief in the city; he had money and jobs to give to his friends and the bottom of the East River for his enemies. Rynders appeared in New York in the 1830's legend has it, having come from an apprentice course on the Mississippi River where he was both a gambler and brawler, expert in the use of either a pistol or a knife. As he became rich and powerful in New York he assigned the chores of fighting and killing to such henchmen as Dirty Face Jack and Country McCleester.

Rynders could start or stop a riot whenever he chose. He made good use of the fact that in its growth, New York had thousands of immigrants of different nationalities, waiting to be exploited and turned one against the other. He also could and did exploit the fact that native born Americans could be turned against all "foreigners." The situation was made to order—and further helped by loosely applied naturalization laws of the day: For a vote, an immigrant could be turned into an American citizen with no trouble at all.

Rynders had only one blind spot, apparently, as he strode through his rough and tumble political career: Being Irish, he hated the English and sometimes he allowed this sentiment to get out of hand. It was Rynders in fact who orchestrated the Astor Place riot against the English actor MacReady. At one point in the three-day-long battle, nearly 15,000 people jammed the streets at Rynder's bidding and only the rifle fire of the Army's Seventh Regiment finally dispersed them.

On less emotional occasions, Rynders displayed real political acumen, however, and when other gang riots seemed to be causing the harassed police undue discomfort, Rynders would pass the word and have it stopped, but always with a reminder to the government that his services in this direction had a price attached and that he would call at some later time to be reimbursed.

The system of Watchmen and marshals which constituted the city's police force remained in effect until 1853. The fee-conscious marshals, treasuring their reappointment by political ward leaders, were inclined to assist voting irregularity rather than discourage it. They, and belligerent gang members, served as "poll watchers" and unwelcome voters were intimidated; ballot boxes were stuffed; immigrants were allowed to vote so long as they voted "right." Blackwell Island prison inmates were let out to vote and reports circulated that publicly supported almshouses were filled with quite able people who simply were being supported by the city in return for a proper vote at the proper time.

The rising tide of democratic feeling in the country at large contributed, oddly enough, to much of the political corruption that marked this period. With President Jackson's democratic sweep into office, the spoils system and the power of the ballot box overthrew the patrician rule that had preceded that time. The result was that the revulsion against aristocratic rule produced the strange bedfellows of boss rule and egalitarian ideas, corruption and idealism. But at that time not one whit of such philosophizing as this would have deflected Captain Rynders—or Hell-Cat Maggie, Gallus Mag, or Jack the Rat.

Disease

Cholera, typhus (ship fever), smallpox, yellow fever. The ports of the world from time immemorial have been springboards for epidemics. Ships arriving at South Street came from China, from Africa, from the Indies both East and West, from South America, and from Europe. Sanitation was crude. Medical inspection on most ships was nearly non-existent.

As the immigrants poured into New York they brought sickness with them. In summer, ships from the Isthmus of Panama carrying gold and passengers from the California ports brought yellow fever. And everywhere, in the damp, creviced hulls of the old wooden sailing ships, the rats swarmed, carrying and spreading more disease.

From time to time attempts were made to rid a ship of rats. The approved method was to seal the hatches after setting cyanide capsules to work. The gas evolved, deadly to all life, was supposed to seep into all crevices and kill all rats. Later the hatches were opened and men sniffed the deadly fumes lightly, waiting until they thought the gas had been diluted with air sufficiently to render it harmless. They would then go into the hull and remove the dead rats.

But twenty-four hours after the fumigation, a rat from a neighboring ship could scurry along mooring lines and plop down below deck to begin the infestation all over again.

Of course after a ship had been at sea for months, passengers and crew were anxious to get ashore and stretch their legs. So were the rats. Among the bales of cotton, cargoes of goods, old sails, rigging and all the clutter of the docks, the rats moved with complete confidence, making their way beneath the docks, across South Street and so into the cellars and sewers of the city.

Disease among arriving immigrants was so much a problem, in fact, that early in the century, sick passengers or those believed to have a contagious disease were sent to the marine hospital on Staten Island before the ship was allowed to dock. Even so, immigrants who carried fever or smallpox in initial stages of the sickness escaped notice and walked ashore to become ill or to die later in a crowded boarding house somewhere in the slums of the city.

The fear of epidemic hung over South Street and the business community of the city for many years. For the history of New York City showed that yellow fever, for example, had struck in 1795, 1798, and in 1801. But 1805 eclipsed them all. Yellow fever struck that summer. People who could afford to, fled the city. Those who couldn't died. Twenty-five thousand citizens were affected that year by the disease.

And as the city grew, conditions worsened. An inadequate and polluted water supply, crude sewers beneath the streets emptying the waste into the East and Hudson Rivers carried more than foul odors. They were favorite promenades for rats who lived, then as now, cheek by jowl with men.

In 1819, just as the port was becoming the largest port in the United States, yellow fever struck. And in September, one businessman with offices on Pearl Street, writing to his father in Boston noted: "the alarm of fever has suspended the little business doing, but I hope with the blessing of GOD, confidence will soon return and Business revive again . . . there was but *one* case of Fever yesterday, & *none* today, although the alarm has so much increased, that most of the Merchants, in Water, Front & South Streets, and many in my immediate neighborhood in Pearl Street, between Old

Slip and Wall Street, *the proscribed district*, have removed . . . the injudicious controversy among the Doctors who seldom agree upon medical subjects, have perplexed the public mind, & multiplied the fears of the timid, while there are always some in every community, whose interest is to cry mad Dog at the appearance of a puppy."

To be on the safe side, however, the merchant sent his wife and children out of town. In many cases citizens went to the "country" north of 42nd Street, where air and water were purer. In others, they went to family seats in upstate New York or elsewhere. Summer holidays and visits, in those times, were frequently a necessity for health reasons and family gossip was mingled during the hot months with talk of survival.

Though the doctors of that time did not know the precise causes of the epidemic diseases, they felt that cleanliness (being next to Godliness) would prevent the spread of disease. So their efforts were bent in that direction. The thousands of unwashed immigrants, however, and the citizenry of New York City to whom bathing was only an occasional ritual resisted the efforts of medical men. In this many were successful and managed to contract ship fever, or one of the other epidemic diseases.

As indicated in the letter of the businessman above, one effect of an epidemic, was to bring business activity to a halt. The wealthy merchants fled the city. The poorer stayed and died or underwent prolonged sickness. Yellow fever struck in 1822 and in 1823. In 1832, cholera swept the port and city. Between July and October, 3,500 people died of it. Two years later, cholera returned and took its expected and, at that time, inescapable toll.

Fire

The night of December 16, 1835 was cold: seventeen degrees below zero. What we today call the "wind chill factor" must have made it seem much colder, for a gale force wind was blowing from the northwest. And at some time that night, a fire broke out in the building at 25 Merchant Street. Flames spread quickly to adjacent wooden buildings.

Alarms brought the Volunteer Fire wagons but by the time they arrived, the fire was out of control. Block after block of buildings shriveled, smoked and burst into flame and the flames, whipped by the wind blew sparks to other roofs and porches of other buildings.

The firemen were nearly helpless. Water from the wells in the area was not plentiful. What was pumped up and through the hoses promptly froze. The lower blocks on Pearl Street and Exchange Place were ablaze and the holocaust was spreading south toward Broad Street.

When dawn came, the city knew it was facing a major catastrophe. People from all over the city came to watch the conflagration and the futile efforts of the firemen to stem the fire. Residents of the area fled their homes. Some, when there was time, tried to save their most valuable possessions. Books, papers, jewelry, silver—all were hurried out and stacked in the streets.

Flames crept eastward to the River from Wall Street to Coenties Slip. All through December 17th, the fire roared unchecked. Citizens and firemen crowded the edges of the fire and here and there among them, gang members from the Five Points section looked on the piles of riches in the streets with hungry eyes. Here was a chance that came all too infrequently for them. Looting began. Some of the more ingenious began setting fire to houses themselves, and darting inside to grab what they could before the fire spread too far. One man was caught by a crowd of citizens as he tried to set fire to a house on Broad Street. The crowd hanged him on the spot and his frozen corpse dangled for three days from a tree before anyone had time to cut it down. Clothes, jewelry and silver disappeared from the unprotected piles of goods in the streets. It was a looter's holiday.

For a time, on that December 17th, it appeared that the entire city would go up in flames. Finally the helpless firemen called for assistance and more and more potent efforts were undertaken to stop the spreading flames. Marines from the Navy Yard came with dynamite to clear a wide swath through buildings on the north edge of the gutted area. They blew up the Merchants Building and the Dutch Church on Garden Street plus many other buildings.

The flames, unable to cross the gap, began to subside. When finally the last ember was extinguished and the bone-tired firemen rested, it was plain that the center of the city's business district had been obliterated. More than six hundred buildings on seventeen blocks covering thirteen acres had been destroyed. Damage was put at over $17,000,000. The fire insurance companies could not pay and were forced into bankruptcy. Business came to a standstill.

This great loss to the largest port in the United States and the seat of a great part of the wealth in the northeast combined with other factors in the economy, helped bring on the panic and depression of 1837 which affected the entire nation.

Most of the buildings in New York—particularly the houses lining the streets all the way from the Battery north to 23rd Street were of wood. They were large, three- or four-story, ornate tinderboxes. And the danger of fire was always present. The city had, in fact, a long history of disastrous fires: 1776, 1778, 1811, 1825, 1835, 1838 and on and on.

One of the reasons for later fires was the introduction of gas through city mains to light homes and streets. It was a blessing in many ways, but a source of trouble in others. Another cause of great fire losses was the organization of fire fighting groups.

All of them were on a volunteer basis. Wealthy merchants and low criminal types from Five Points and the Bowery alike were members. Fierce pride was developed and the teams competed with each other to be first on the scene. Each year a Fireman's Parade was a big event in the city and the fire wagons were tended lovingly and polished to perfection. Many were given names: Red Rover, Big Six, Black Joke, Yaller Gal and a host of others. The competitive spirit was strong and the reputation of a particular fire brigade was the most important thing in life to many of the brigade members; so important in fact, that putting out the fire became of secondary importance. When an alarm sounded, the honor went to the brigade that got to the scene fastest—a laudable aim. For the brigade that got there first, and got its hoses turned on the fire before any other, was *ipso facto* the winner. And since there were only a limited number of fireplugs or wells, he who got to the fireplug or well first, usually got the prize. The inevitable began to happen: The alarm sounded; the fire laddies leaped to the heavy man-drawn wagon and began tugging it through the streets to the cheers of onlookers. If two brigades met and one blocked the other's path, a fight ensued then and there. The more competitive intelligences at work on the problem realized that the key to success was the fireplug nearest the scene of disaster. So they sent a large, muscular representative of the brigade running ahead of the wagon with a barrel. He would arrive at the fireplug in question, clap the barrel over it and sit on it. If another brigade arrived first, the barrel-sitting fireman would fight to his last ounce of strength to prevent their use of the fireplug until *his* brigade arrived. Meanwhile, of course, the fire blazed on, a matter of no real importance to the buffeted and buffeting firemen.

The Similarity of Then and Now

Like a ghost image on a television screen, the history of South Street walks beside contemporary events. For the same problems seem to be scattered across today's newspapers and reports that puckered the brows of civic leaders in the heyday of New York's growth. If one fixes attention on the colorful though not always genteel events of the first half of the nineteenth century, the picture of that time glows brightly but it is followed relentlessly by our memory of today's news. Schools, crime, water supply, street cleaning, gangs, overworked police and the unending power struggle between city and state government haunted the byways of South Street then as now.

In 1813, the state of New York allowed public school money to be spent on parochial and other religious and private schools. Its dispensation was entrusted to the Common Council—a governing body of the city. The Council allowed money to be spent on several independent School Societies as they were known then—but refused to give funds to any sectarian schools. The problem simmered along and in 1840 the Catholic Free Schools applied to the Council for funds. Public school administrators protested and the Council denied the use of public money to support parochial schools. A citizen today would have to admit there is a haunting similarity to such a controversy.

The problem roused so much controversy that in 1842, Governor Seward and the Legislature created a law that placed the public schools of the city under state control. Each ward was considered a "township" in the state's eyes insofar as school organization was concerned. Still, no state money was to be spent on religious schools. The state allowed local administrative control of schools, however, and that question seemed to be resolved.

What we define today as crime in many cases was, in South Street's heyday, merely accepted behavior among the "lower classes." Drunkeness, sexual assault, pilfering, robbery, even murder often went unpunished by a weak and ineffective police force. In the case of murder today police launch an investigation that might continue for many months. It was difficult in 1850; such an investigation could not be carried out since there were too many distractions—meaning additional murders. It was somewhat like trying to fix your attention on one mosquito and catch it as it darted among a whole swarm of them.

Increasing crime today brings forth statements in New York that exactly parallel the thought, if not the impassioned words, of an Aldermanic Committee report in 1844 which read in part: "Witness the lawless bands of ruffians that stroll about our city, the gamblers, the pickpockets, burglars, incendiaries, assassins, and a numerous host of their abettors in crime, that go unwhipt of justice, and we find indeed that it is true that something should be done to tie more efficiency to our laws and protection to our unoffending citizens!"

The city police today work long hours, are undermanned, and in the future may succumb to an occupational malady: deafness caused by hearing the precinct station phone ringing without end to report more work to be done. The work load is a common complaint of police and it surfaces from time to time as cries for efficiency, more police, and the rising tide of crime hit the pages of the newspapers.

Police of 1850 and earlier were equally overworked. In 1844, in fact, the system of Watchmen and fee-collecting marshals still remained. Efforts were made that year to modernize the rickety and amateurish system. The reform was to occur when the Mayor and the ruling Common Council gave their approval. But since the reorganization scheme had come from the state legislature—and city-state relations were as strained then as now—the Mayor and the Council were somewhat laggard in putting their signatures on the documents. Still it was clear something had to be done. So, acting as though the legislature did not exist, the Board of Aldermen proposed its own plan which involved merely updating the old Watch system. Among the Board's recommendations was that the Mayor outfit the Watchmen with some sort of badge or uniform to distinguish the men from the ordinary citizen. To everyone's dismay, the Watchmen refused to accept the uniform. Their argument reflected the strong democratic tides that were unseating the old patrician order of things: They claimed to be free and equal citizens of the Republic and didn't want to be seen going about dressed as liveried servants.

The closing months of 1844 saw a great deal of backing and filling as the city's leaders struggled with the problem and finally, in the spring of 1845, the city gave in and adopted the plan put forward by the legislature. The city was divided already into political wards and these in effect became the "precincts"—each with a captain and assistant captain. But right there and then, the problem of overworked police began. In addition to watching the city both day and night, the police also were expected to be poll watchers during elections, light the gas street lamps, sound alarms, and inspect streets. With any stray minutes left they were also to act as health and fire wardens, dockmasters, and to inspect public conveyances.

The police reorganization plan of 1844 fumbled through the next decade without noticeably improving matters. The Captain Rynders of the city were increasing, not only in number but in the power they exercised. The struggle in the city then was not between the "good guys" and the "bad guys" but between rival factions of thoroughly "bad guys." In 1854, Fernando Wood was elected mayor. Astute, apparently honest, he gave a brief flurry of hope to reform-minded, conscientious citizens. But during his administration everything seemed to come unglued. He wore the mask of virtue, but during his time, corruption reached new heights.

The state government realized that the times had offered the state an opportunity to increase its control. New York City appeared to be facing an almost total breakdown of "law and order" as well as the dispensation of essential city services. So the state moved to take the power of government away from city officials. The state revised the charter of the city. The state separated the Mayor and another key official from the county government structure. Another reorganization of the police department ensued— but more importantly the control of the police department of New York City passed from the city to Albany. The Governor and the State Legislature passed and approved all of these reform measures. But alas, Governors and state Senators were as human then as they are today and possessed less than Olympian judgment. They forgot that when authority outside a community is exercised on the community, nearly all warring elements within the community close ranks and attack the alien force. As might have been expected, riots broke out. Mayor Wood refused to turn over the police force even though the state Supreme Court had validated the actions of the state government.

For a time there were two police forces in the city: part of them submitted to state jurisdiction and part of the force remained "loyal" to the city. This strange state of affairs came to a head in mid-June of 1857 when Mayor Wood literally threw a state-appointed Street Commissioner out of City Hall. The bruised Commissioner got a warrant for the Mayor's arrest. Loyal city police prepared for the siege of city hall as loyal, state-approved police attacked. The gunfire rattled in the vicinity of City Hall as policeman fired on policeman.

In one of those curious and amusing coincidences of history, the Seventh Regiment, kept in trim by battling rioters here and there in the city, happened to be parading down Broadway enroute to embarkation and departure for Boston. As police gunfire began to drown the music of the marching band, it became evident that more than the musical services of the regiment were once more in demand. So the Seventh Regiment put down a final riot, a true police riot, by the way, since no one but police were involved.

30

There are today a host of irritations between Albany and City Hall in New York. And it is plain that long before the famed Lindsay-Rockefeller feuding and caterwauling broke out, the City and State of New York lived at best in a state of uneasy truce. The cries for "local control" and fair amounts of state aid for city tax money paid echo back in time to prove, once again, that nothing changes.

2

Shipbuilding

I f South Street was a forest of masts and rigging looking down the East River, it was apparently an endless series of shipyards looking up river. In the 1830's, shipyards lined the East River
from the foot of Pike Street to Corlears Hook and round, out of
sight all the way up to Thirteenth Street. Schooners, ships, barks,
brigs, steam sailers, and later iron-hulled steamships all came down
the ways of East River yards.

As many as 33 shipyards were busy in the thirties, forties and
fifties, some of them large even by today's standards. In the later

thirties, for example, John Englis opened a yard at the foot of 10th Street that employed 450 workmen and covered 140,000 square feet of space. His specialty was steam sailers and by 1866 he had built over fifty such vessels.

The beginnings of the shipbuilding frenzy in New York's East River can be traced in the circumstances of the War of 1812. England's overpowering navy blockaded the major ports of the United States. Such ships as sailed, had to hazard a passage during darkness in or out of the port. If daylight came before they were clear of the coast, speed and sailing skill alone could save them. Of course, not all escaped. This meant that the young United States had to replace the sunk or captured ships by building them in U. S. ports. And in the meantime it had to start almost from scratch to build a Navy.

It was during those frantic years that some of the original great names of American shipbuilding came to the fore. Christian Bergh was one such man. Tall, six-feet-six, meticulous in his construction of ships and a man of wealth as a result, he undertook the building of several ships of war for the Government in the infant Brooklyn Navy Yard across from South Street. On completing these, he was sent to Lake Erie to construct more war ships there. When the war ended, Bergh opened his own yard with offices at the corner of Scammel and Water Streets. Legend comes down of his care for detail. One morning in the thirties, he was said to have been sitting in his office, watching a workman shape a timber some 150 feet away from his window. The man put down his tools when he had finished. Bergh leaned out of his office window and called to the man, "That's three-quarters of an inch out of line." Then he ran downstairs and spoke to the workman in what were reported to be warm tones about his sloppiness. The workman swore the beam was all right and appealed to the two other owners of the yard. To settle the matter, the beam was carefully measured and, sure

As many as thirty-three shipyards like this one supplied packets, clippers and coastal vessels for the growing trade of the port. *Reproduced through courtesy New York State Historical Association, Cooperstown, New York.*

enough, it *was* three-quarters of an inch off the horizontal. Understandably, Christian Bergh thereafter was regarded as one having the "eye of a hawk."

But it was just such exactness, such care for detail and for precise work that made America's reputation for shipbuilding. No other country during that time built better ones. Other builders, then and later, took as much care and it was on this quality plus innovative design of ship hulls, that reputations and ensuing wealth were built.

To insure such precision, skilled shipyard workers endured a long and difficult apprenticeship. It was a voluntary slavery, in fact, in which a young man put himself if he wished to learn, as the saying went, "the art, trade, and mystery," of shipbuilding. Among other things, the apprentice agreed not to marry. He also agreed not to gamble, not to "haunt ale houses, taverns, dance houses, or playhouses." He could not go anywhere, day or night, without getting his "master's" permission; he could not buy or sell anything without permission.

In return, the master agreed to teach the young man his trade. And he further agreed to pay the young man $2.50 per week plus an allowance for room and board if the apprentice were not living in the master's house.

Such an apprenticeship lasted three or four years. It was the hard but necessary trade school of the day. Upon completing his apprenticeship the young man could apply for work as a "mechanic" in a shipyard. He might be a ship-carpenter or a blacksmith but whatever his trade, the day was long, the work backbreaking and the pay meager.

The working day early in the nineteenth century was from sunrise to sunset, six days a week. That meant in summertime that the men worked from four o'clock in the morning until nearly eight o'clock at night. At eight each morning the men went home for breakfast. At noon, there was a two-hour dinner break. They needed all the nourishment they could get for the machinery of shipbuilding consisted principally of the workers' arms and strong backs. Huge beams were manhandled into place. Only later were poles and derricks rigged with block and fall to raise large heavy timbers to their positions.

Beams, planking, and all other wooden members were cut by pit sawing. With the log in place over a deep open pit, and six men on top and six down in the pit they worked a huge handsaw up and down squaring the log into a desired beam. The pitmen, as the lower team was called, wore netting over their faces to keep the sawdust from choking them but that was about the only concession made to their comfort, if not survival. Fifteen hours a day, six days a week these sawyers worked. Today the monotony and mind stultifying dullness would not be tolerated anywhere but on Detroit's car production lines.

Save for the breakfast and dinner breaks, the only relief men got during their work day was at eleven in the morning and four in the afternoon, when "Grog break" came. For three cents, workmen could get a drink of brandy and there were few who didn't take the opportunity.

Wages for the men were at $1.25 a day for many years—which with a fifteen-hour day comes to less than 8½ cents per hour. In time, pay went to $1.75 per day but the hours, not the money was what caused the most anguish among the men. They struck, finally, for a ten-hour day. Shipyard owners offered them $2.00 a day if they would continue to work fifteen hours, but the men had had enough. Ten hours became the rule.

So pleased were the men, that they paid for a bell—called the Mechanics' Bell—which was placed in a tower on Lewis Street between Fourth and Fifth Streets, and paid a bell ringer to ring it at seven in the morning, noon, one o'clock, and six. With the new schedule, the men could live a little less arduously, a little more like human beings. Breakfast could precede the start of the day's work instead of interrupting it. The midday meal break was cut to one hour and with everyone through at six, a relatively lengthy evening stretched before the men.

This increase in leisure time, not much by today's standards, was put to good use by the men, all of whom lived in Manhattan within a few miles of the yards. During lunch hours, or after closing, they rowed across the East River to Williamsburg—then largely rural with fruit and vegetable gardens. There they bought vegetables and fruit from the gardeners or farmers, and filched a few free items from trees and gardens along the shore enroute back to their boats. Incredible as it seems to us today, the East River was swimmable then. Above Thirteenth Street was a jut of land called "Dandy's Point" and there the men and their wives or girl friends went swimming from a clean beach of white sand. They arrived on summer evenings in wagons, changed clothes behind shrubbery and romped into the water. Their bathing costumes were not swim suits, but older clothes which the water would not damage.

For evening entertainment, there was the East River Garden, a

Fishing and swimming in the East River, unthinkable today, was a favorite pastime for shipyard workers over a hundred years ago. *Courtesy South Street Seaport Museum.*

combination beer garden and play house (apprentices not allowed). A section of the Garden was roofed over and a stage had been built. On it, the owners presented melodrama of the period and choral groups from time to time. Independence Day was celebrated by shipyard workers who joined the traditional parade with a forty-foot model of a ship on miniature ways about to be launched. The "float" was on wheels drawn by horses through the bannered streets while young workers dressed as sailors helped with the pulling or walked alongside waving to admiring crowds.

Apprentices, bound as they were to work not play, frequently burst the rigid strictures of their contracts and, being young, raised a little cain of their own from time to time. One group of apprentices was housed in a boarding house built by their employer, Noah Brown—of the builders Adam and Brown. This house became an unofficial center for planned shenanigans and one of the apprentices' frequent pranks was to steal out at night and change the signs on storefronts so that a grocer's sign might appear on a barbershop the next morning. They might be forgiven such small failings for they were learning one of the most demanding trades of the day under a discipline that few people today would submit to.

Building a Ship

Today, with measuring instruments that can determine the wavelength of light, we tend to think that in "cruder" days things were built by little more than guesswork. But a wooden sailing ship, constructed by a master builder in a New York yard was a precise work of art in which each plank and timber was planned, drawn and cut with almost a cabinetmaker's care.

At the height of the shipbuilding era in New York, the narrow streets leading to the East River yards were jammed with workmen early every morning but Sunday. Ahead of them rose the great rib cages of ships, tall-sheers or masts with block and tackle dangling from their tops. As they approached, shed roofs came into view and the great stacks of timber of many kinds: oak, elm, locust, ash, yellow pine. The air, in those early morning hours was filled with the smell of freshly cut wood, of pitch and tar, the smell of iron and of burning coke in a blacksmith's forge.

Caulkers, sawyers, carpenters, blacksmiths, helpers, axmen—all the trades of shipbuilding were represented in the crowd of men. And when they arrived, each at the place he had occupied the day before, the sounds of work rose with the morning sun.

Long before a ship began to be built, its designer, a naval architect, had spent hundreds of hours producing the model, the drawings, and figuring dimensions that were to be reproduced, lifesize, in the yards. A series of thin cedar and pine boards from three to six feet long dowelled together gave the architect an oblong mass from which to cut the model of the ship. With supreme care, the hull shape was produced in miniature. Under the skilled hand and eye of the architect it seems to emerge from the mass of wood he shapes. Every line, every measurement of the finished hull is produced exactly in the model. When the model is complete, the architect begins to produce the critical drawings that will be used to determine the dimensions of each piece of wood going into the ship. The main one is called the shear drawing and it is composed of three parts: shear plan, half-breadth plan, and body plan. The shear plan shows the hull as though it were cut from stem to stern and looked at from the side, the body plan, as if it were cut across at the widest part of the hull. The half-breadth plan again is a cut from stem to stern, but now looked at from above the deck. One by one the detail drawings are made and the thousands of parts, large and small, dimensioned and numbered.

Given such plans, any shipbuilder anywhere in the world could produce the finished product. In this case, however, the plans are studied by one or more of the yard owners—themselves sometimes naval architects or master builders. The working master builder in the yard studies the plans, too, and when he is finished, the work is begun.

At the very outset, blocks are laid on which the keel will rest. They are put down carefully on a slight slant, tipping toward the water. The usual degree of tilt was 5/8 of an inch per foot of keel length. So, from the start, preparations have been made to launch the ship when she is completed.

As the days pass, the workmen swarm over the growing ship: first or false keel, keel, stem, sternpost, cross-pieces, futtocks, top timbers, floors, half floors, shelves, beams.

The pitsawyers work cutting the timbers. The top men, visible to everyone, bend and straighten, bend and straighten all day like rocking horses. Great oak logs are wrestled into place over the pit, and squared off, twenty inches on a side. Holes bored out with a long auger are readied for scarphing or dowelling. Huge sledges drive copper bolts deep into and through great timbers. Axmen cut notches and long grooves in tough oak, the shining blades of the great broadaxes flashing in the light and striking the same place on the timber each time with great accuracy.

The ship frame rises, looking like a dinosaur's rib cage and then begins to disappear as planking goes in place. To meet the demands of the hull's changing shape, going from bow to stern, the planks are placed in the steambox until they are flexible enough to bend easily. They are fastened to the frame members by "tree nails" of locust wood. Inside the inner planking goes up and hides the iron network trussing that gives strength with flexibility to the entire hull. But before any planking goes on at all, the master builder carefully checks to see that the frame is vertical and true—for once the planking is in place, the shape is set. Should the master builder discover the frame to be leaning a bit one way or another, he orders the iron trussing rods tightened on one side and loosened on the other to bring the frame to its true position.

Caulkers swarm along the sides of the hull as soon as the planking is in place. Their mission is to make the seams watertight. Using hemp threads from old rope, called oakum, they drive the threads with caulking irons into the plank seams. When this is done, the seams are covered with hot pitch which soaks into the threads and covers the seam itself.

Rudder, capstans, tiller, tiller ropes, blocks, wheel. Copper sheathing eventually will protect the hull, and caulking of inner planks will complete the waterproofing job. But these two final steps to protect the hull are often not taken until the ship has been in the water a voyage or two. Masts, spars, and rigging come later, after the launch. As the ship is readied for her entry into the East River there is genuine excitement for all the workers, the yard owners and the ship owners. For the launch is the end of a job for most of the mechanics who work there. The ship's owners begin to plan profitable voyages; yard owners think in terms of being paid for the job.

Preparing the ship for launching is not a simple matter of buying a bottle of champagne and handing it to the owner's daughter to break over the bows. Ways must be laid—smooth planks reaching from the lower end of the blocks supporting the ship to the water at low tide. The slant of the blocks is increased from 5/8 of an inch per foot of length to 7/8 by wedging up the bow and reducing the thickness of the blocks toward the stern. The keel rests on the blocks first laid down, and the hull is supported on either side by bracing and the whole forms a cradle to keep the ship upright.

A single timber called a dog shore is propped under the stern and held in place by a heavy wooden cleat. It keeps the ship from slipping into the water unannounced. As workmen prepare the

41

Launch of the *Challenge* from a South Street yard near the midpoint of the nineteenth century. Workers and owners shared a half-holiday celebration complete with band and drinks. *Courtesy South Street Seaport Museum.*

ship for launch, other activities are going on in owners' offices. Flags and bunting are broken out and begin to cover the ship. A band is ordered to appear before launchtime; punch, beer, rum and champagne are ordered by the case and food is prepared.

Despite the shipyard owners' protests, the ship owners themselves insist that the workmen be given at least a half holiday for the launch. The costs of the party are borne willingly by owners, but the builders see only a half-day's work lost forever.

On the ways, men slather grease to assure a smooth run into the water. A line is attached to the dog shore so that at the signal to launch it may be pulled away, freeing the ship to enter the water for the first time.

When launch day arrives, the excitement is at its height. The band arrives. Cannon are loaded for an initial salute as the ship heads for the water. Brandy passes freely among the men—as do rum, and beer, and gin. A stand has been built running within reach of the ship's stem and to the cheers of workmen, the owners, shipbuilders, and the girl who will christen the ship mount the stand.

After the speeches, the music starts up again. The builder leans over the rail and shouts "Down dog shore." The trigger is sprung as the line pulls the dog shore from its position. The young lady breaks the bottle of wine just as the stem recedes from her. And the cannon begin to fire as the band plays as loud as possible to be heard over the cheering.

A number of things could happen to spoil the occasion. Supports might give way at an awkward moment, allowing the ship to roll over on its side in the mud on the bank—a most inglorious beginning. Or, it might slide so swiftly down the ways that it gained enough momentum to send the ship across the East River into the farther shore. Usually, however, the passengers on the decks going for the ship's first "ride" had little to fear. Even more important, no mishap would mar the holiday atmosphere.

And there were "perfect" launches. As one man aboard a ship that had such a perfect launch wrote of the vessel's movement, "A slight jar, a rush to the sides, roar of cannon, loud huzzahs from outsiders, Dodsworth's Band playing 'Departed Days' and through the portholes it was seen that the vessel was in motion. So gentle and steady was the movement, so slight was the dip, and so gradually was she brought up by her anchors before passing twice her length from shore, that a person standing on board, with closed eyes, could not have realized that any change whatever had been made in her position."

From 1833 until 1860, with only two exceptions, the New York Port led all U. S. ports in tonnage of ships built annually. But it was during those years that the era of wooden sailing ships came to

43

a close. Steam sailers, developed as far back as the first decade of the nineteenth century, gradually displaced sails. Iron hulls replaced the wooden frames and planking. And when that displacement was nearly complete, the arts and skills of shipwrights departed with the wooden ships. The commerce of the world never again would depend upon sail and wood, but steam and iron. Here and there in backwaters and among enthusiastic yachtsmen, wooden ships had a place. But the large shipbuilding centers echoed to the rivet gun and the hiss of welding torches rather than the mallets, axes and saws of the great days of sail.

The Builders

Many of the most famous shipbuilders in the history of South Street underwent the years of apprenticeship and became "mechanics" like many workmen. But having become skilled in the shipbuilding trade, they were not content to stop there and spend the remainder of their lives as hired laborers.

Christian Bergh—he of the hawk eye—was one such man and he was among the earliest successful builders in New York's history. The War of 1812 brought him contracts for ships and an assured place in history. With all his wealth he lived and worked as he put it "a Democrat." His home remained on the corner of Scammel and Water Streets and his office was in his home. All his life he could look from his windows to the shipyard. Though urged often to run for public office, he always refused. Building ships was what he knew and what he did. His belief in the simple life of a true democrat never wavered and in his later years his reputation for honesty and fair dealing was citywide. Even the politicians respected him. One of Christian Bergh's accomplishments was to be the first shipbuilder to employ blacks in his yard.

Henry Eckford, a Scotsman, was a friend and competitor of

44

Christian Bergh. He too rose to prominence in the War of 1812. His first yard was on the Brooklyn shore and it was there that he built the famous ship *Beaver* for John Jacob Astor's farflung trading empire. During the War he went, as did other builders, to the Great Lakes region to build ships there and protect the young Republic's northern boundary from British invasion from Canada. Immediately after the War he temporarily became Superintendent of the Brooklyn Navy Yard where his passion for honesty collided with the favor-granting so common in Government organizations. The Commodore's horses needed shoeing, and he asked the men in the blacksmith shop to do it for him. Eckford was passing the shop when the horses were being shod and he instantly ordered the horses removed. "The business," he said, "of this shop is to repair Government vessels, not to shoe Commodore's horses."

Like Bergh and Eckford, the young firm of Adam and Noah Brown helped build warships on the Great Lakes. They also built privateers that harassed the British during the years of conflict. One, the *General Armstrong*, achieved a measure of fame by turning the tables on the blockading British Navy. The warship crossed the Atlantic and blockaded an English port for a time—to the horror and incredulity of the English citizens.

As the older builders approached retirement, they looked more keenly at the young men they took on as apprentices. The skills learned over a lifetime of shipbuilding ought, they felt, not be lost and they determined to train bright, upcoming young men in all the mysteries of the art.

Among the apprentices of Eckford, two became outstanding shipbuilders: Isaac Webb and Stephen Smith. These young men went on to found dynasties of their own. Webb and Allen became a famous yard as did the builders Smith and Dimon. These builders grew up in the era of fast packet ships and they built many of them as well as cargo vessels for the growing China trade. Their careers

45

spanned both the rise and the peak of maritime supremacy of the United States in the middle years of the century. Packets and clippers represent the apogee of sail and both firms built their share. Stephen Smith's yard built the packets *Independence* and *Roscoe* and later two famous clippers: *Rainbow* and *Sea Witch*. Isaac Webb's yard built the two largest merchants ships in the United States at the time: the *Superior* and *Splendid*. Unhappily they were too large. No cargo could be found in sufficient quantity to give them profitable voyages. So one of them, the *Splendid*, was converted to a packet liner for the Havre run.

Jacob Westervelt served his apprenticeship under Christian Bergh. And for a time he worked in Savannah, Georgia building ships there. Christian Bergh had no intention of letting the young man get away, however, and he invited Westervelt to join his company. During those years with Bergh, Westervelt and the other partners built most of the packets that came down the ways of New York yards. Westervelt was well thought of in the city and became Mayor of New York in 1852. His real vocation, however, was shipbuilding and when he left office he received the contract to build a steam frigate, *Brooklyn*, for the U. S. Government.

Through all the years of the supremacy of sail, steam sailers were developing slowly. There were many problems. Sidewheelers or stern wheelers were the first means of propelling the ships by steampower. But with the invention of the screw propeller, the steamship was in business.

One of the earliest builders with an interest in steam propulsion was John Englis. A native New Yorker, he was born in 1808 and served his apprenticeship in the yard of Stephen Smith. He rose to the foremanship of another New York yard and, in 1837, went to the Great Lakes, where steam shipbuilding was flourishing. He built two ships there, the *Milwaukee* and *Red Jacket*. Then he returned to New York, as knowledgeable a builder of steam vessels

46

as existed at that time. He opened his own yard and the production of steamships rose. In less than a thirty-year period, John Englis built fifty-six steamships.

Englis had the mania for speed that was later to infect the entire country. By today's standards, his ships were not very fast, but one he built, the *Sumo Nada*, made the 1,000 (nautical) mile run from Hong Kong to Shanghai in fifty-six hours. This was an average speed of a little over 20 knots, which *is* a good speed today and was an exceptional one then.

Many of the steam sailers designed then were destined for protected waters since sidewheelers or stern wheelers could be easily damaged by the large waves of the open sea. In 1863 Englis built the *St. John*, first of the palatial river boats at a cost of $600,000. Its run was New York to Albany and it ushered in the famous coastal or river-cruising ships of the latter part of the nineteenth century. His yard also built the *Newport*, which began eight-hour service from New York to Newport, R. I. then approaching its zenith as a fashionable summer vacation region.

Bergh, Isaac Webb, Stephen Smith, Henry Eckford, Noah Brown, John Englis. Their names and others make up the roll call of the great American shipbuilders who catapulted the young United States to the top of the world's maritime shipping heap. Yet none surpassed the son of Isaac Webb, William H. Webb, a man of extraordinary energy and ability.

William Webb was born in 1816. By 1831 when William was fifteen, his father had become financially successful as a shipbuilder and he was determined that his son would not have to enter the difficult and exhausting business of building ships, whatever the money to be made. Money was no problem then for the Webb family. So Isaac had plans of a more easeful life for his son, travel, culture, social graces, a suitable display of wealth in the rising city of New York. There was only one drawback to Isaac

Webb's plan for his son: William H. Webb was born to build ships.

In 1831, at the age of fifteen he became an apprentice with all the backbreaking work that entailed. He sawed, he planed, he doweled, he pulled his weight with all the other workmen in the yard. And he learned the ancient art of shipbuilding. On the Fourth of July he could be seen, dressed as a sailor, pulling the shipwrights float of a model ship on ways in the usual celebration.

When he had learned the physical work of shipbuilding, he went into the mould loft, the drawing room, the model room of his father's headquarters. Here design, intuition, knowledge all joined to produce improved hull and rigging design. And William learned that critical part of the business.

As his father grew older, William singlehandedly designed some of the last ships built by Isaac Webb. In 1840, William Webb was in Europe when word reached him that his father had died. So, at the age of twenty-four, William Webb took his father's place in the firm.

Like John Englis, William Webb was interested in steam. He also was interested in building warships. In 1847, he built the *United States*, a steamship designed primarily for carrying cargo and passengers, but capable of being converted to a warship in a crisis. The *United States* could carry enough coal to make the entire Atlantic crossing under steam alone. She was the first steamship to enter the San Francisco harbor through the Golden Gate. And her design and speed even in the roughest of head seas impressed many people. In 1849, he built the *Guy Mannering*, a three-decker packet which carried many immigrants from Britain to South Street piers. In the following ten years, 126 ships came from the yard presided over by William H. Webb and it would seem he had reached his goal of shipbuilder supreme.

But he still wanted to build warships. The United States Government refused to give him a contract in 1851, so he informed the Russian Government that he was available to build a battleship for their navy. The result, finally, was the *General Admiral*, 325 feet long, a beam of 55 feet, a depth of 34 feet and mounting 70 guns. Her sailing character was impressive. Under canvas alone in a good breeze and with her propeller lifted clear of the water to reduce drag, the *General Admiral* averaged twelve knots. Her power plant was huge for those days: two horizontal engines of 800 horsepower each.

The U. S. Government began to regret that they had turned down William Webb. As soon as the Russian warship proved itself, the British Government quickly built two ships based on Webb's model; U. S. officials inspected the *General Admiral* and decided they were looking at a better warship than they had seen before.

Rather than wait for the Government to make up its mind, Webb signed contracts to build two iron-sheathed steam-frigates for the Italian Government. The only U. S. contract Webb had managed to get was for a Revenue Cutter.

The shortsightedness of Government is legendary. Yet it seems incredible that Washington did not invite suggestions from William Webb to build warships. The clouds of the coming Civil War already loomed on the national horizon. Webb had built an outstanding warship for Russia made of wood and steam powered. He was building ironclads for Italy and keeping far ahead of anyone else in the technology of warships, engine design, armament and all the other skills the Government would need so desperately in the months ahead.

The famed battle of the *Monitor* and *Merrimac* was history when William Webb got his warship contract. The ship was a steam ram, named the *Dunderberg* and she was not launched until 1865. The *Dunderberg* was a unique vessel even when compared to the *Monitor*. Her length was 378 feet, beam 73 feet, and the depth of her hold, 23 feet. The *Dunderberg* had sides that were five feet thick, protected by iron sheathing five inches in thickness. Her engines, all below the waterline, developed 1,200 horsepower and the revolving gun turrets and their naval rifles could fire shells weighing 500 lbs. She was truly the first "modern" battleship.

William Webb, one of the last great shipbuilders longed to build warships. He got his chance with the heavily armored *Dunderburg* launched near the close of the Civil War. *Courtesy South Street Seaport Museum.*

William Webb was very nearly the last of the great shipbuilders of South Street. There are many reasons for the decline of shipbuilding in New York following the Civil War. One of them was rising land values along the shore that made large shipbuilding space prohibitively expensive. Wooden ships could be built much cheaper on the coast of Maine where land was plentiful and wood grew just behind the yards or at best only a few miles away. Another reason was the Civil War itself. Confederate raiders captured and sank a lot of Union tonnage and this discouraged investment in ships and shipyards. The shift from wood to iron also had its effect. After the Civil War, high tariff protected the infant U. S. iron industry but it raised costs on the building of iron ships to an unrealistic point. William Webb himself complained in a letter to a friend, in 1869, "My business is destroyed by the absurd law of a high tariff, which destroys the shipping interests—the right arm or bower of our country." Yet another factor helped kill shipbuilding in New York: Large iron-hulled ships carried so much more cargo than wooden sailing vessels that the number of ships needed to carry on commerce was drastically reduced.

The end of the golden era of shipbuilding was at hand and with all the reasons for its decline listed above, perhaps one of the most subtle but decisive was the fact that the sons of wealthy shipbuilders no longer lived in offices near South Street, adjacent to their yards. Direct supervision twenty-four hours a day vanished as the wealthy sons moved farther and farther uptown. These young men did not care to tap the secret of William Webb's success: Attention to detail. For William Webb, shipbuilding was life itself. He marked every stick of wood that went into his ships, he fussed all the time over details. He was in his yard in early morning darkness long before the first sleepy-eyed worker entered the cluttered grounds. And he was always the last to leave at night. As darkness closed down he could be seen marking or measuring or simply standing in the dusk, dreaming of another ship to build.

3

The Ships

THEY WENT ALL over the world, the ships. Launched from the yards along the East River they sailed to the Indies, Caribbean, China, Europe, the Arctic and even the Antarctic regions. In that time, maritime supremacy came to the United States. And in that time, the shipbuilders of South Street led all others in the nation.

Life in the sailing ship days is probably best glimpsed in the reading of whaling voyages, of the logs of ships setting out from

New York, or New Bedford, or Salem, or New London for a year, two years. What of the whaleships, cruising the Line (Equator) in the Pacific ten thousand miles from wife and home and family? Or was this so? Not quite.

Four years a voyage might last, with no sight of home port. But in the Pacific, one ship would 'speak' another, back sails, drop off a boat and spend a day or two gamming: crew gossiping with crew; officers with officers. And one or the other of the ships had left port last. And one or another was outward bound, another homeward bound. Letters might be exchanged. The homeward bound ship took messages of cheer to families on Cherry Street or Scammel, or Madison, or East Broadway. The outward bound ship might have letters for crew members of the earlier departed ship. A Post Office on the trackless wastes of the sea!

Thousands and thousands of square miles of the huge Pacific Ocean, turned into a lake by American ships. No one can read Herman Melville's early books without being struck by how frequently people, and ships crossed and recrossed each other's paths. The Marquessas, Tahiti, The Sandwich Islands—and Melville ducking the law in one place or another, having jumped ship and in another place, having engaged in a "mutiny."

The fast China clippers, the packets to Havre and Liverpool, smaller ones to Havana. Around the Horn to San Francisco and the Gold Rush. New York papers carrying all news of passages, gold strikes, and who was returning from the gold fields, a millionaire.

The nineteenth century saw the ultimate design of commercial sailing vessels. It also saw their end, as steamships and the screw propeller proved faster and more dependable than reliance on wind alone. Today the art and skill of designing, building, and sailing wind-driven vessels is confined to yachting. Here and there a few Navies still train their midshipmen in sailing ships and the ports of the world are occasionally treated to the romantic spectacle

A lyric of canvas, the full-rigged ship personifies the great days of sail. South Street yards then built more tonnage than any U.S. port. *Courtesy South Street Seaport Museum.*

of a square-rigged ship moving majestically toward another land-fall.

The names, styles of rigging, and abilities of the sailing vessels were numerous and no young man in or near South Street in 1850 would admit to not knowing them all—in many cases not only by type but by individual name. Like young men of today who know sport car types, young men then knew the difference between ship, bark, barkentine, brig, brigantine, schooner, and sloop. And each rig, for various reasons had its purpose and period of popularity. Our vision today of that great day of sail almost invariably invokes a picture of a full-rigged ship, all sail set, going off the wind at a prodigious rate. This might be the clipper ship of legend and pop-ularity in the public mind.

This picture, however, is only a partial one. Somewhat less romantic is the picture of a full-rigged ship, with sails slatting in the doldrums, wallowing about in flat water, unable to catch any wind to take her in the direction she wants to go. In such a case, the other extreme of sail rigging might have been more efficient, at least more picturable. The schooner, with sail rigged fore and aft, along the line of the ship's length, could catch light breezes and sail closer on the wind than a square-rigged vessel. In such light airs as held the square-rigger back, a schooner might move gracefully on a desired course closer to the wind.

Schooners, rigged fore and aft, have been used as work-a-day fishing boats from time immemorial and as yachts by the wealthy. *Courtesy South Street Seaport Museum.*

All other sail rigs are merely combinations of these two extremes. If the mizzen or aftermost mast were rigged fore and aft while the two forward masts, fore and main, were square-rigged, the ship was a bark. If only the foremast were rigged square, and the other two fore and aft, she became a barkentine. Two-masted vessels were brigs and brigantines. A brig was rigged square, a brigantine with the foremast square rigged and the main fore and aft. In America such a rig was termed hermaphrodite.

Two-masted hermaphrodites or brigantines were used by the Revenue Service which was the forerunner of the Coast Guard. *Courtesy South Street Seaport Museum.*

A square-rigged ship, like the clipper of our imagination, could not be beaten when she sailed off the wind. Then, all her sails were working at their most efficient. To tack or point at all into the wind, the yards holding the sails in place had to be braced or swiveled around so that the wind would fill them. But of course there was a limit beyond which yards would not swivel, and this limit defined the ability of a square-rigger to sail into the wind.

Nowhere in sailing history have the advantages and disadvantages of square-rigged ships shown themselves more clearly than in the schedules and courses of the packet ships perfected in the first half of the nineteenth century. The packets themselves were at first not large vessels, not over 400 tons displacement, nor more than about 130 feet long.

At first, simple trading vessels that were fast were pressed into service on the first packet liner service to Europe. But as the demands of the competition for speed and sturdiness became evident, designers produced blunt-bowed, relatively light, securely braced ships that gained fame in the constant crossing and recrossing of the Atlantic.

The times of their crossings are an indication of the square-rigged ship's efficiency. Going from New York to Liverpool, for example, the first packet to sail, the *James Monroe* in January, 1818, reached Liverpool in 25 days. The westward bound "sister" ship, *Courier* set sail from Liverpool one day before the *James Monroe*. In the westerly winds and winter gales, it took her 49 days to reach New York.

The reason for this difference lies in the prevailing winds which blow from west to east. Thus the *James Monroe* was going off the wind all the way and in this situation her three masts carrying square-rigged sails operated best. Heading west, into the wind was another matter. The *Courier* in its westward passage had to tack across, bracing her yards to their extremes to catch wind.

Sailors grapple with the huge sails of a packet in a blow. Winter crossings brought storm and hazard to crews of such ships. *Courtesy South Street Seaport Museum.*

The packets, when they were fully developed, were the pride of the sailing world. Designed for passengers and "fine freight" such as silver, silks and other expensive but non-bulky cargo; they were trim, well-kept and sailed by the best captains and crewmen in the maritime world. If a captain would not put on all canvas to make fast passage, he soon found himself relieved of his command. And crew were expected to make or furl sail fast when the first mate bellowed an order in the teeth of a north Atlantic winter gale.

Not at all strangely it was the clipper ship that caught and held America's imagination, apparently for all time, as the triumph of ship design. As a matter of fact the clipper ships were built and sailed to gain only one of the three fundamental elements that determine ship design: speed. The other two elements, cargo capacity and economy of operation, were sacrificed in the clippers. So as "best all around ship" the clipper was, curiously, a failure. The chief difference between clippers and packets was the length to beam ratio and the bluntness or sharpness of the bow. Both were full-rigged ships but the clipper in its race to capture the China tea

58

market from English competitors, was sharper in the bow, had a higher length to beam ratio and was as lightly constructed as possible. In fact, the longer, leaner look caused a serious deficiency in the hull's strength or ability to withstand storm waves and the endless buffeting by the rolling seas.

If packet captains were harsh masters, clipper captains were worse. And if crews aboard packets had to brave north Atlantic gales, clipper crews had to furl or make sail as they rounded Cape Horn beating westward through Drake's Passage where the worst storms and largest waves in the sea are found. Average wave heights in that dread stretch of water are forty feet, crest to trough, and considerably higher when storms sweeping across the South Pacific push countless tons of water into the relatively narrow "channel" between the tip of South America and the Antarctic's north reaching Palmer Peninsula.

In that wild waste of water, the long, lean clippers were at a disadvantage. Many were dismasted, many sank without ever being heard from again, and nearly all lost sail after sail as the captain held as much sail aloft as he could, driving westward to the broad Pacific.

Yet clippers caught people's imaginations then much as space vehicles now fascinate the population. The exploits of clipper captains, the ships and the fastest passages were known to every school boy just as our astronauts are now. For who could resist such names as *Flying Cloud* and *Sea Witch*? Or the thought of a sail carried above the topmost skysail—and called the moonraker?

The era of the clipper was short, running from about 1846 to 1859. Two factors ended the exciting era of the clippers. The first was the increasing emphasis on speed from the ship. The clipper design sacrificed everything to gain speed and so produced, finally, an uneconomic vessel. The second was the ascendancy of steam.

Steamships of course had been around a long time—since the

Clippers rounding Cape Horn often suffered the fate of this ship. Storms ripped canvas and toppled masts, leaving a tangle of rigging behind. *Courtesy South Street Seaport Museum.*

first decade of the century. But the early successful ones were side or sternwheelers that were suitable mainly for river, lake or inshore voyages. The use of steamships (with auxiliary sail) on the high seas was restricted until the development of the screw propeller in 1836. The advantages of this form of force application to the water soon produced what we know essentially as the modern steamship. And that marked the end of the clipper ship era.

In addition to the two ship designs, packet and clipper, that were built in South Street yards and elsewhere, there were many smaller craft: Pilot boats (schooner rigged); brigs for coastal and West Indies trade; steamships for river traffic and barges for the Erie Canal; sloops and small schooners for fishing boats.

A packet or a clipper, when built was given a useful life expectancy of about seven years. If the ships were still floating after that time, they went into less demanding work as traders wandering to all the ports of the world in search of cargo. Then as steam took over and the shipbuilding business moved from South Street to the coast of Maine, the remnants of the great age of sail subsided on reefs and mudflats up and down the coasts of all the countries of the world. Their last cargoes were high bulk, low cost materials such as nitrates from Chile, timber from Newfoundland and Maine, copra from the South Seas.

As late as the 1920's, there were still wooden hulls moving slowly across familiar seas. But by that time they had become so rare that upon sighting them men ashore or in modern passenger liners stared for hours at the tall masts, the weathered sails, and the planked hulls, until at last they disappeared, hull down, over the horizon, gone forever.

4

The Merchants
of South Street

THE MERCHANTS of South Street were a rare breed. Their word was their bond, literally. They ran great risks. When they succeeded they made great profits. If they failed, they took their losses. If those were too great, they were forced out of business.

Most of them came from New England. They all made decisions singlehandedly or in informal consultation. They knew the sea and they knew ships. For them, business often was a great adventure,

62

like the one that befell Edward Knight Collins one bright day in 1825.

On that day, the Liverpool trader *Canada* sailed up the East River bringing passengers and cargo to New York. In addition, the *Canada* brought some interesting news: The price of cotton had skyrocketed in England. This news set in motion a chain of events that catapulated E. K. Collins to the top of his business.

At that time the source of most of England's cotton was the southern-producing states in America. New York merchants had been trading with southern planters and cotton brokers and frequently exports of cotton from the port of New York were greater than exports from southern ports such as New Orleans and Charleston.

The *Canada* had no sooner docked than South Street merchants and some speculators saw that an opportunity was at hand. The news from England was worth a fortune, and everyone knew it.

The speculators immediately booked passage on the packet which was due to sail for Charleston that same day. Their aim was simple: Get to that cotton port and buy up all the cotton they could. Several South Street merchants wanted to do the same thing. That meant they would have to send someone as their agent to Charleston and get there before the speculators. The man they chose to be their agent was Edward Knight Collins, junior partner with his father in the firm of I. G. Collins and Son. E. K. Collins listened to the merchants' story and offer and when he was asked how soon he could set sail, the twenty-three year old young man said, "As soon as I can charter a pilot boat and ship provisions and crew—about three hours. I will be ready to sail at four o'clock this afternoon."

The merchants pointed out that the regular Charleston packet would sail at the same time and they also pointed out that the packet, carrying more sail than any ship Collins could get, would undoubtedly beat him to Charleston. To this, Collins replied calmly, "Gentlemen, I will go in the way I have named, or not at all."

The Charleston packet let go her lines at precisely four o'clock, leaving from Burling Slip. The large three-master stood out in the East River and to the amusement of the speculators on board, E. K. Collins set sail at the same time in his small chartered pilot boat. It looked like a hopeless race to the merchants.

Collins busied himself stowing provisions and clearing his little ship for sea as the two vessels went through the Narrows. Whatever else his activity accomplished, it allowed him to ignore the laughs and comments of the men on the larger ship. He had a small vessel with light draft and not much sail. The speculators had a full-rigged ship. How could he beat them?

In his own mind, E. K. Collins had already answered that question. He was a young man familiar with ships. He was an excellent navigator and he knew exactly what to do.

As the packet drew off outside Sandy Hook, her sails filling in the brisk wind, Collins let her go her own way. He set a course inshore where the shoal water was no hazard to him but where land winds, tides, and currents along the coast could be caught. Catch them he did. The packet disappeared to seaward and Collins sailed his little boat south, fast.

He beat the packet to Charleston. When he landed, Collins bought all the cotton in the city and contracted to buy from planters whose cotton fields stretched along the rivers behind the town.

Sailing back to New York, he entered the harbor just as the packet was returning with the disappointed speculators and as he conned the little pilot boat across the bar, the men on the packet watched him without offering any comments about the "boy" who was setting out to do a man's job. He'd done it.

Like many merchants in New York, E. K. Collins had a New

England background. His mother died shortly after he was born and he was raised in Truro, Massachusetts by an aunt. He "finished" school at fifteen and was hired as a clerk in a store owned by a Mr. McCrea and a Mr. Slidewell. It was located at 41 South Street. A five-year apprenticeship brought him a position with John F. Delaplaine and he sailed several times to the West Indies in his employ. Shipwrecks, adventures with pirates, and knowledge of the sea came to E. K. Collins during those years and when he was 23, he became a junior partner in his father's firm. The offices were on the corner of South Street and Burling Slip. It was to this office that the merchants came to ask his help in beating the cotton speculators.

By the time E. K. Collins established himself under his own firm name, the packet service to Europe, begun in 1818, was well established. Collins felt in 1830 that he had yet to gain the financial strength to challenge existing lines. So he did the next best thing, he started a line of coastal packets that sailed regularly between New York and Vera Cruz. These were full-rigged ships. He next started sailing packet schooners to Tampico from New York. And soon after that, a line between New York and New Orleans.

Most of Collins' ships were built by the yard of Brown and Bell. But E. K. Collins controlled their design. He was himself a proficient naval architect.

In 1833, the *Mississippi* was launched from the Brown and Bell yard. It was 750 tons and could carry 2600 bales of cotton. The ship was designed by Collins and was the largest vessel in existence flying the U. S. flag. In 1834, Collins paid for a still larger ship, the *Shakespeare*. She sailed at first to New Orleans and caused considerable comment. Not only was the *Shakespeare* large, she looked like a man-of-war. Then the *Shakespeare* picked up a cargo in New Orleans and sailed for Liverpool. Her arrival caused a stir in the great port. Her size and different design drew crowds and the Captain, John Collins, uncle of E. K. Collins, unloaded his cargo, called police to handle the curious crowds, and for a week he held open house aboard the large, new ship. When the *Shakespeare* sailed for New York, she had to turn down a large number of passengers who wanted to take passage on her and the captain had to reject a lot of cargo also.

In New York, the report of the *Shakespeare*'s success, prompted Collins to finally enter the transatlantic passenger and cargo trade. His line, called the Dramatic Line, had as its symbol on the foresail a large cross shaped like an X. The Black Ball Line, first of the packet lines, with its huge round black circle on the foresail had another competitor.

Earlier than most merchants and ship owners, E. K. Collins recognized that steam was going to displace sail. In 1840 he made the decision to build steamships in the future that would make the crossing to Liverpool in not more than ten days. It took him until 1850 to keep his promise to himself but in the years 1850-51 four steamships became the mainstay of his transatlantic fleet: *Arctic*, *Pacific*, *Atlantic* and *Baltic* were their names.

By this time, E. K. Collins had become the outstanding merchant-shipowner in New York.

From the beginning of modern New York, the principal business was trade. The merchants originated, directed, and controlled trade and so they became the natural leaders of the city.

Tody, in an era of corporate managers, who move from company to company in their journey up the ladder of success, it is difficult to imagine the respect accorded the merchants of the first part of the nineteenth century. But in contrast to today's business directors, men like E. K. Collins served long apprenticeships at sea, in the shipyards, as clerks in various firms. And as their names became known and trusted by the community, they rose by a natural process to found their own businesses. Their character, their personal honor, their social and private lives were all associated with the firm name. If any one of them stumbled in any area of living, the firm suffered a loss of reputation.

There were two aspects of business then that required absolute honesty of the merchants: credit and religion. Most of the business conducted from day to day was done on credit and promissory notes. And in this business the Federal Government played an im-

Stevedores unload ship cargo on South Street docks. Trade was the life-blood of New York and merchants developed it. *Courtesy South Street Seaport Museum.*

67

portant part. In the 1820's the United States was facing competition with all the established countries and governments of Europe. England in particular had become the great empire building trading country that led all the rest. In the face of such competition it seemed to U. S. leaders that to grow and become a mature nation and economy, the promotion of the general welfare required that the Government give the merchants a good deal of help.

The Government did this in the form of credit. Advances were made and payment required so that a merchant could send a ship to China and have it return with a valuable cargo of tea and spices before payment was due. In this way many fortunes were made.

The risks of credit were as hazardous then as now. So intricate was the exchange of notes, so elaborate the system, that the failure of cotton firms in New Orleans could set off a local panic in New York—and firms would fail there as a result. We hear little of those failures today but a typical one, noted in history only because of the future fame of a son of the family was that of Alan Melvill, or Melville as it was later spelled by that famous son, Herman Melville.

Allan Melvill, of upper class Scottish ancestry, was an importer in New York. Never in the front rank of merchants, he owned no ships but relied on brokers in France to supply him with "fine stuffs" of silk and delicate design to be sold to wealthy New York buyers.

His business flourished at first and he moved with the growth of the city during the 1820's from adequate but unfashionable locations toward what then was believed to be the "better life." His record shows moves from 6 Pearl Street to 55 Courtlandt, to Bleecker Street, and finally to Broadway, where, as Allan Melvill wrote to his relatives, his wife Maria had always wanted to live.

He found that as his immediate success continued he could get credit for ninety day periods. With luck he could dispatch an order to France, have goods shipped to him and bank the selling price before his note came due. But the plagues which struck the port of New York often suspended business as families fled to the safety and cleanliness of the country. Occasional downturns in the business cycle kept creditors from renewing Allan Melvill's notes. He borrowed from his father and he borrowed from his wife's brother —all the time giving the usual outward signs of affluence and well-being. Then the roof caved in. His ninety day credit was reduced to forty-five days. In 1830, his business failing, his creditors knocking on his door, Allan Melvill admitted defeat and planned to return to Albany, his wife's home town.

He left behind unpaid bills and this panicked the always excitable Allan Melvill. He wrote to his brother-in-law, Peter Gansvoort, about the remaining creditors who were closing in, "After having commenced this suit, can they now molest me at Boston or elsewhere out of the state?—in what time can they recover judgment? . . . Can I not give a Bill of Sale of my furniture to JM in part payment of my debt & secure the use of it by a lease from him?"

Poor business judgment, uncontrollable variables in the business climate, shipping losses, all of these things combined at last to show Allan Melvill that credit was a two-edged sword.

The linking of religion to business profit has a long history. In those years of the nineteenth century the belief that God favored the upright merchant, and punished the sinful, was at its height in American history. And there were, as might be suspected, prayers of hope and prayers of thanksgiving freely mingled with business letters and documents.

The minor but turbulent business career of Allan Melvill produced a great number of business letters of this nature. They are frequently sprinkled with such terms as: "Under the blessing of Heaven," "merciful Dispenser of all blessings," "with the blessing of GOD, confidence will soon return & Business revive again . . ."

In the belief that God played a direct, discernible part in business affairs, Allan Melvill was not alone. Ship owners, risking everything on a single cargo from some distant land, thought long and gloomily on the hazards and storms of seafaring. Most of the front rank merchants had come from the sea themselves, as captains or mates of vessels that sailed all over the world. They were well aware of the whimsical nature of sea disaster. And so they frequently composed bills of lading that began "Shipped by the Grace of God in good order and well conditioned." These bills of lading then ended with the heartfelt sentiment that ". . . God send the good ship to her desired port in Safety. Amen."

The opening of the Erie Canal in 1825 was cause for a giant celebration. New York merchants early saw the Canal's advantage and profited by it. *Courtesy South Street Seaport Museum.*

The vision and foresight of the great successful merchants cannot be denied. They saw the advantage to the building of the Erie Canal. And when it was completed, their trade and profits grew. They vigorously exploited the so-called Cotton Triangle and controlled many Southern plantations and brokers by extending the all-pervasive credit of the times to them.

In 1849 gold was discovered in California. Though far removed from the actual gold fields, New York merchants made profits on that discovery. The newspapers of New York in that year and the following ones carried long and detailed accounts of the riches that were being dug out of the ground three thousand miles away. The *New York Herald*, for example, in its issue of December 9, 1850 bore this major front-page headline:

Arrival
of the
STEAMSHIP EMPIRE CITY
with
Over Two Millions of Gold Dust
and
THREE HUNDRED CALIFORNIA
MILLIONAIRES

The report included news of cholera at Sacramento City and also contained a list of marriages and deaths in the "Gold Region."

The gold rush was important to New York merchants because the quickest way to get to the gold fields was by ship to the Isthmus of Panama and then across it to another ship sailing for San Francisco. The ships, of course, were owned by New York merchants. And there was profit, too, in cargo as well as passengers. In 1849 prices in San Francisco had climbed so high that in themselves they were news to be carried in New York papers. Flour was fifty cents

71

a pound and brandy (sold at three cents a glass in New York) cost twenty-five cents a glass in California. Lumber, pork, bread—all the necessities for existence—brought huge prices and merchants in New York benefited.

So, with holds stuffed with food and building materials and liquor, decks crowded with would-be millionaires, the ships set forth.

The steamer *Hartford* departs South Street for the California gold fields in 1849. Merchants quickly began supplying ships and food for the journey. *Courtesy South Street Seaport Museum.*

There was also a shortage of skilled workers in San Francisco and the gold-dust minded Yankees set out to remedy the situation. Shipyards lost workers to the lure of gold. One vessel arrived in San Francisco with sixty-four trained men: carpenters, blacksmiths, mechanics. On the long voyage to the Golden Gate, these men managed to make their own cots, tents, and hammocks. They had built a boat (it might be useful). They made knives from old files (and inlaid the handles with pearl from oyster shells). On deck they had set up a blacksmith shop where they could make or mend anything they wanted to. The captain of that ship, *The Oxford*, arrived in San Francisco in a state of nervous collapse. He had been worried, he said, for fear the men would cut up his ship, masts, spars, sail and all, to make things they thought of. The Yankees who descended on San Francisco went right on being ingenious. One picked up discarded packing cases and sold them; another painted signs on canvas and sold them. They were young men, determined to be merchants but needing money to get started. And many of them did. One young man returned to the East Coast a few months later with $13,000 worth of gold. He banked it and headed right back for more.

Two wars bracket the era of the great South Street shipping merchants: The War of 1812, immediately after which, the first great merchants appeared, and the Civil War, whose damage to the merchants and to U. S. shipping in general proved fatal in the years since that destructive conflict. Disruption of shipping during the war was unavoidable but it would seem reasonable to expect the merchants to recover and return to their profitable business. A number of changes, however, occurred during the period of the Civil War that altered the entire climate of the New York port. Iron ships, for one thing, were replacing wooden ships—and New York did not have iron available as cheaply as wood. This meant that merchants like E. K. Collins could no longer work side by side with shipbuilders to get the vessels they wanted. And during the war, foreign shipping gained a lead that was difficult to overcome. Another change was the telegraph and the transatlantic cable, oddly enough. With Europe linked to the U. S. and every city in the U. S. in instant communication with each other, price information that spelled profit for the discoverer of it vanished. If everyone on both sides of the Atlantic knew overnight of price changes, no advantage could accrue to a particular merchant and the price of cotton in England automatically affected the selling price in Charleston, South Carolina.

5

~~~~~~~~~~~
~~~~~~~~~~~

Immigration

On the base of the Statue of Liberty on Bedloe Island there are inscribed the famous words:

> *"Give me your tired, your poor,*
> *Your huddled masses yearning to be free,*
> *The wretched refuse of your teeming shore,*
> *Send these, the homeless, tempest tost, to me*
> *I lift my lamp beside the golden door."*

The men, women, and children from all the countries of Europe who accepted the invitation flooded into the port of New York by the thousands. More of them arrived at South Street piers than at any other point of entry. And they were, the "wretched refuse" of Europe's teeming shores. War, pestilence, depressions, political turmoil, famine in any or all European countries from time to time acted as a spur to drive people to the new world where dreams of land, of freedom from the economic slavery of Europe's rigid caste systems were to ease their suffering.

From 1820 to 1860, the total arrivals of "alien passengers" reached nearly five and a half million. Of this number as many as 98 percent, by one estimate, were immigrants. A few came as cabin passengers—either to visit or to settle as wealthy colonists. But by far, the majority were drawn from the "huddled masses." The peak year prior to the Civil War was 1854 when over 450,000 immigrants came to U. S. ports. More than 320,000 of these landed at New York.

And while South Street, for that great number of people, may have been "the golden door," it was neither reached nor breached without hazard, discomfort, and deception.

The old immigration, prior to 1860, drew nearly all of its participants from The British Isles, and northwestern Europe. The two countries contributing the greatest number of immigrants for many years were Ireland and Germany. In the peak year of 1854, 176,000 Germans and 82,000 Irish came to New York City either to stay there or to travel inland via the Erie Canal to lands of the opening west. The year before, the two nationalities had been almost neck and neck in the numerology of arrivals: 119,000 Germans; 113,000 Irish.

Immigrants, of course, had been coming to the new world ever since the first colonists landed and formed communities. But as the shipping routes developed between Liverpool, Havre, and other

European ports and the eastern seaboard of the United States, the tide began, slowly at first, to increase. By the time trade had created a wealthy class in New York it began to occur to the merchants that there was a fortune to be made in shipping more than cotton, textiles, flour, or other products. They saw they could make money shipping live human bodies. And they began to harvest the human crop.

In this they were assisted by landlords and government policies abroad. An Irish landlord, for example, in a famine year might find a considerable number of his tenants starving to death and begging him for food. If he did not provide it, they turned to the parish authorities and so reduced the church's treasuries. The pauper Irish tenants were a drain on profits; and what was worse, threatened to dip into the landed gentry's capital. And so the word of immigration to the United States was spread by many "brokers" who posted signs in the cities and towns and countryside of poor lands occupied by poorer people. These signs told of wealth, farms, freedom, food, employment, equality, and justice to be found in the United States. As precursors of Madison Avenue hucksters, the brokers were already well advanced in the arts of deception and misrepresentation. Each broker, of course, received a commission on the deliverance of a pauper to the Liverpool docks with passage money, his family, a bundle of rags for luggage and the dream of good things to come firmly implanted in his head.

Jobs were promised glibly, and such was the condition of many English, Irish, and Germans, that they fell in the broker's hands with the ease of ripe apples falling from trees in a high wind. In some cases the poor, the old, the sick, were gathered together by famine-struck parishes and shipped out at the expense of the parish. The authorities felt that it was worth the expenditure to get rid of them.

Average passage cost was twenty dollars a head plus a small allowance for clothing and food which each immigrant family had to take aboard ship with it. Children under fourteen were counted as half adults for cost and so the business flourished.

In Germany, caravans of immigrants made their slow way across country to ports in Germany and France. The story there was much the same as in England, Ireland, and Wales. Get rid of the poor, the huddled masses, they're cutting into our profits.

On the U. S. side, businessmen sensed the growing market and sent brokers out with instructions to sell, sell, sell. And sell they did. One unhappy arrival in New York City complained that brokers in Ireland had plastered handbills on every tree, street corner, and in every pub in Dublin. All the main towns of Ireland, the complaint went on, had at least one busy broker, urging people to leave their homeland and go to America where jobs were plentiful.

Here and there among the landlords and gentry of England and Ireland, there were men who showed humaneness in dealing with their departing tenants. One Mr. Vere Foster, for example, financed the emigration of over 15,000 women to America out of his own pocket. Tenants from the estate of the Earl of Egremont in Sussex fared better than most. The Earl paid the entire cost (passage, food, clothing) for those of his tenants who chose to leave.

As the floodtide increased, Immigrant Societies formed in Scotland, England and Ireland did what they could to make the transplantation less hazardous. Yet these efforts numbered only a small percentage of the total.

Most immigrants had never seen the sea nor more than a picture of a ship. When they were evicted from their small cottages, they packed and bundled their meager belongings onto carts and wagons and headed for ports like Hull, and Leith, and Cork. The flood tide grew until, in 1851, people were leaving Ireland at the rate of 5000 per week. Liverpool was the chief port of embarkation for the new world, however, and there the conditions were at their worst.

Waiting at the ports to greet the emigrants, were boarding house "brokers," and merchants prepared to sell anything to the country bumpkins who were as bewildered as sheep in their strange new surroundings.

All ships, except the regularly scheduled packet liners, sailed when the captain had a cargo and felt like sailing. A trading ship might advertise departure but there was no assurance it would leave on the designated day. Hence, emigrants would arrive at a port, pay for passage on a ship and find that three days, a week, a month might pass before they actually sailed. And so the boarding houses along the docks did a thriving business. Most were never clean; none was large enough. The result was that, according to one account by an eyewitness, as many as forty people of all ages and both sexes would be put in a single room furnished only with dirty straw to lie on. If one of the "boarders" wanted a blanket, he was charged for it. Food supplied was bad and expensive.

Before many days had passed, the average emigrant family found itself paying all or most of its small store of money to stay alive until the ship sailed. Under these harsh conditions, far from a poor but orderly life on a farm, the family as a source of strength, love, and unity began to break down. Men were persuaded that liquor would prevent seasickness; and teetotalers took to drink. Destitute of cash, wives and daughters in formerly respectable families began earning money as whores.

Food and clothing for the voyage had, in most cases, to be purchased by the emigrants themselves. And here was another method of fleecing the already partially sheared sheep. As the days passed in port, however, most families found they could not afford to buy special clothing for the journey. For those who could, one adviser suggested "the kind of apparel I would recommend to male passengers would be short jackets or waistcoats with sleeves, a dark handkerchief for the neck and coarse trousers." He further suggested that women take "a long bedgown or wrappers with dark shawls or handkerchiefs as cleanliness cannot be observed with any degree of precision." Which was an understatement.

Food was a more pressing problem. The westward passage might be as short as 30 days; on the other hand, storms and head winds could increase the passage to more than ten weeks. So the emigrants were advised to take enough food for their family or group for ten weeks. Unfortunately not everyone had money enough to do that. And they were at the mercy of merchants doing business at the port. Salted beef, for example, which was one common staple food for the voyage, often was sold in casks. Advertised and sold as freshly salted meat, the beef frequently proved to be two or more years old. It soon became spoiled and the affected emigrants had to go on short rations. Potatoes, a staple for Irish emigrants, frequently rotted in the dampness aboard ship.

Advice on the kind of food to take, and the quantity was plentiful. Among the items not usually considered were pepper and mustard in plenty—to mask the taste of rotting meat; vinegar in quantity, to hide the taste and smell of the drinking water. On better ships it was possible for emigrants to take live pigs, chickens and ducks for eating on the way. On others, steerage passengers were allowed to hang cured beef quarters in the rigging—although there was no guarantee whatever that the crew or other emigrants wouldn't steal it. On the average ship, however, all food taken by emigrants had to be stowed in steerage with the passengers.

As stories multiplied about emigrant troubles aboard ship, following passengers took heavy locked boxes in which to keep food. They kept their boxes locked, and kept the key on their persons at all times. For when it was clear that the voyage would be a long one, the poorly provisioned passenger found himself and his family face to face with starvation. And in those circumstances, stealing food inevitably became the lesser of two evils.

80

Emigrants crossed the Atlantic in all types of ships. In the 1820's —before the trade in emigrants was recognized by New York merchants as a profitable business possibility—no special ship was used. Emigrants booked passage on anything that lay in port. Fishing boats from Newfoundland would take a few people; the fast sailing packets also took some but most space aboard these ships was designed for cabin passengers, and high fares. In the early 1830's, shipbuilders began producing "emigrant ships" designed to stuff as many bodies as possible into the steerage. Cargo vessels of all types improvised spaces to take aboard human cargo as well as the usual amount of freight.

Most ships had two decks. The top deck was open; the lower one built in some five and a half feet below the top deck. It was on this lower deck, stretching nearly the length of the ship that emigrants made their home during the crossing. Below the lower deck, in the bottom hold of the ship, cargo was stored. The ordinary cargo ship was not designed with two decks and the lower one, when added, was of a temporary nature. For if the next voyage dictated an entire cargo of inanimate freight, the lower deck could be removed.

Other discomforts came from the attempt to convert regular cargo vessels to emigrant ships. Since the ship designers had not counted on human cargo, no toilets and no washing facilities were available on the lower deck. Nor was there any provision for ventilation of the between-deck space. The only way to get any fresh air in there was to leave the few hatch covers off. In stormy weather of course, even this could not be done. Emigrants remained battened down between decks for days as Atlantic gales spent their fury on the ship.

The question of the number of emigrants allowed aboard any given vessel was usually never seriously considered. As the flood increased—and with it the profits of shipowners—the question became academic. True, Governments tried to establish space requirements per steerage passenger, but such regulations were easily and frequently broken. Between-deck steerage space aboard the average cargo vessel was about 75 feet long, 20 to 25 feet in width (varying along the hull line) and only 5½ feet high—where the beams of the hull did not reduce it even further. On some ships, rows of plain wooden bunks were placed on either side of a long five-foot wide aisle. Only about eighteen inches of vertical space separated the bunks. On other ships the bunks were ten feet wide and five feet long to accommodate six adults.

Government regulation tried to establish the rule that one steerage passenger only be allowed for every two tons of cargo space. This was later changed due to the outraged cries of the shipowners, to three steerage passenger for every four tons of cargo space. Since adults were the basic unit of figuring, children under fourteen were counted as half an adult; those under seven, a third; those under one year old were not counted at all. So the cargo tonnage of a vessel did not automatically tell officials how many emigrants were loaded onto the ships.

Even when regulations were enforced in port by the few and indifferent inspections of officialdom, captains could sail from Liverpool, or any other port, with the regulation load of steerage passengers, put in another port or pre-appointed spot, and pick up a hundred or more clamorous departing Britons. In the 1840's and early 1850's, even top deck space was sold, so that hundreds more undertook the long voyage on the open deck exposed to the weather and with little hope of protection when storms struck.

The emigrant ships were so bad in the 1830's that one knowledgeable passenger later wrote, describing it as "a tub of a vessel, without a sailing point in her composition. . . . Water tanks, heaps of biscuits, barrels of pork and but one of rum; a pennant, an ensign, a skipper, a fat mate, and a superannuated lieutenant of the navy by way of agent, and a most inadequate crew, were put on board, and the transport was reported fit for sea."

As for inspection of the vessel, in 1850, in the greatest port of departure, Liverpool, a total of six men superintended inspection of 568 ships which carried more than 174,000 emigrants. Whatever the law, the means to enforce it never were provided.

German ships sailing from Bremen or Hamburg were in much better shape than British ships. And American ships, for the most part, were the equal of the best ever to carry emigrants. By the mid-1840's, American shipbuilders had begun to supply better steerage passenger ships. By then, the East River shipyards had turned out ships specifically designed for steerage passengers. One, built in 1843, had three decks, well-ventilated in the between-deck spaces and reasonably equipped with heating and toilet facilities. Yet the cruel overloading, bilking, and misrepresentation was the main feature of the average ship in the first half of the century. Conditions aboard them were, as one writer finally put it, as bad as on the slave ships operating from the coast of Africa.

Before steam-powered tugs and harbor vessels were developed, the emigrant ships lay to at anchor offshore. In the case of Liverpool, in the Mersey River, launches and small boats took passengers to the ship's side to load them and their belongings; later, steam tugs would take the fully laden ships down the Mersey to favorable winds and a last glimpse of the land.

Sailing dates, as previously mentioned, were lackadaisically adhered to and although emigrants might be in Liverpool, presumably ready to board the ship at quayside, many frequently were startled and nearly left behind when the captain, in his whimsical authority, decided that *now* was the time to leave. One newspaper account of departure indicates the confusion and excitement and unpredictability of the event.

Of 385 passengers whose fare had been paid to cross the Atlantic, 360 were Irish emigrants. On being advised that the ship was to

Emigrants from Ireland and England struggle to board ship in Liverpool. Hundreds of thousands left poverty and a cruel caste system to search for freedom and dignity in the New World. *Courtesy Museum of the City of New York.*

sail, they began clambering aboard with chests, barrels, boxes, and all imaginable sorts of gear. Without checking to see if everyone was aboard, the captain ordered lines cast off so the tug could tow the ship down the Mersey to catch the wind. Over fifty paid passengers had not yet boarded ship. They came flying to the dockside, tossed bundles on deck; some bundles fell into the water where they were hauled out and passed up by a small boatsman. The men leaped the widening distance between ship and shore, the women screamed, hesitated and finally threw themselves at the ratlines where some dangled ingloriously upside-down, their legs "sadly exposed to the loiterers on shore." A drunk tried the leap, missed, and fell into the water from which he was indecorously hauled aboard.

In the case of another ship, the scene was almost the same, and one passenger wrote of its departure, "Some of the emigrants might be seen gazing on the nimble sailors running up the shrouds, creeping along the stays, and lying out on the yardarms. Some were lingering on shore, to drink a farewell glass with their friends; and others were making merry on board, at the prospect of leaving Britain and its oppressions, their griefs and sorrows behind them, and entering upon a land where sighing and suffering, want and misery, were believed to be unknown."

In the romantic view of history, emigrants setting out to settle new lands are seen as the lean, young, tough, adventurous souls that have often been shown in Hollywood movies on the subject. But if there was an overall, average emigrant to be described during the later phase of the "old" migration during the first half of the nineteenth century, that picture would have to be of a debt-ridden pauper, middle-aged or older, unhealthy, and burdened by an equally downtrodden wife, and surrounded by four, five or six thin children of which he was the father.

Chances also were great that he could scarcely read and write.

All his life he had been ordered about and when he had dragged his luggage and family below deck to the steerage quarters he simply tried to make the best of things, which, aboard ship, were not very good things. Unless some more intelligent and humane passenger was present among the emigrants to organize the mob, he had to fend for himself and family. Yet even among the lowest of the emigrants, there was the sustaining faith in a better life ahead; certainly not one as bad as that left behind.

A few lamps lit the dim interior of the steerage quarters. The aisle between bunks quickly became clogged with food boxes, cooking utensils, clothing bundles and whatever small mementoes the women had salvaged from their abandoned homes. In the spring and summer months hatches were left open, but in winter they immediately were shut and the air became foul. As soon as the ship reached the open water, its rolling produced the inevitable seasickness and with the inevitable results. Children cried. The lack of toilets soon became woefully apparent and before two days had passed, all had been initiated into the unbelievable hardships of emigrant passage to the land of the free. The golden door might be beckoning but the cost of getting to it was proving higher than anyone had believed possible.

In many ships there was no separation of the sexes. Thievery in the semidarkness, assaults upon unprotected women and girls all became commonplace—and none had yet to deal with either the captain or the crew.

Ships were required by law to carry enough fresh water to supply each passenger with a gallon a day. But if overcrowding raised the vessel's cargo above the legal number, there was correspondingly less water for each one. This meant no bathing whatever on many passages to the west. It is little wonder that disease broke out; sickness increased where it had existed before and frequently fever would strike down scores of the crowded weakened emigrants. If deaths occurred, and they frequently did, the remains of the emigrant were unceremoniously committed to a watery grave.

One writer described the ship's officers and crew and the ship itself in unflattering but highly accurate terms. The average such vessel, he observed, was "little better than a hermetically sealed box; as deep as it was long, with clumsy square bows and stern, with ill-cut, ill-set sails—its standing rigging of hemp a mass of long splices. . . ." As for officers and crew, they were, he tartly reported, rum-soaked, illiterate, bear-like officers, who could not work out the ordinary meridian observation with any degree of accuracy, and either trusted to dead reckoning or a blackboard held up by a passing ship for their longitude."

At sea, a ship's captain is traditionally elevated to the stature of a deity. His word is law. All appeals for the legal ration of water—or of food if passage included that—had to be made to him. Many captains abused their power considerably. One steerage passenger watched in amazement as the steerage passengers were brought to the upper deck for their water ration only to be kicked and abused by the mates and sent below again when only thirty of several hundred emigrants had been given a little drinking water.

On ships where emigrants had to supply their own food, stoves were set on deck and lighted at specified intervals for cooking. Emigrants crowded upon each other trying to heat a little oatmeal, or soup made of salt beef or bacon. On better ships a regular routine was established either by the captain or some more intelligent members of the emigrant group. The best organized and most comfortable passages were undoubtedly those on which an Emigrant Society had chartered the entire steerage space and sent an organized group aboard under selected leaders from among the members. The worst voyages were made by ships that carried the hordes of Irish during the potato famine from 1847 to 1854.

Whether a vessel was among the best or the worst of ships, its human cargo had three tremendous hazards to face in the crossing: storms, fire, and disease.

Any westward passage made during the winter or early spring months was almost surely to be a long one, accompanied by storms. To the women, the children, and to all who had never sailed at sea before, a gale was as terrifying an experience as they had ever undergone. At the first dash of spray over the side, hatches on the steerage quarters were battened down and the three, six, or nine hundred landlubbers were sealed in their box. There, for days, in utter darkness, since neither candles nor lamps were lighted in such conditions, the women shrieked, the children screamed and at every roll or pitch of the ship, they believed the ship was sinking.

Wrote one passenger of such a storm, "Ship quivering, masts creaking, pumps going. The ship now seemed perfectly unmanageable. The water poured down in torrents. The condition of the women was especially deplorable; one told me she had not been in bed for four nights, and had remained all that time in her wet clothes . . . The women were screaming at a dreadful rate . . . Death appeared now certain."

Disease could strike the healthiest, best-managed group who ever set sail from Liverpool. Smallpox, cholera, and "ship fever" or typhus could and did take their toll. The crowded and unsanitary conditions of the average ship reduced the health of everyone so that the weakest among them fell prey to whatever germ was carried aboard by a sick passenger or, in the case of typhus, came from the hordes of rats that infested the lower holds of the ships.

Shipwreck and fire at sea were twin hazards faced by all emigrant ships. Cleanliness and medical inspection (very late in coming to steerage passengers) could have cut down death by disease. But even the best of wooden sailing ships could founder at sea with tremendous loss of life. Icebergs, storms, a lee shore, any of these or a combination would splinter the hull, dismast the ship and bring its own form of disaster. Most ships carried only a few lifeboats. Rarely more than four. These were for the crew and cabin passengers; the human cargo in steerage was considered expendable. So little was a human life worth in those days that one newspaper account of a disaster reported that "twenty souls and 240 emigrants were lost."

Fire in a wooden ship was a constant hazard. And when a fire started—whether from an immigrant's careless smoking below deck, an overturned lantern or candle, or spilled embers from a cookstove, the results frequently were dramatic and catastrophic.

One vessel, just out from Liverpool in 1848 caught fire and although two nearby ships offered assistance, great numbers of emigrants died. An eyewitness account by a man on a relief vessel wrote, "The flames were bursting with immense fury from the stern and center of the vessel. So great was the heat in these parts that the passengers, men, women, and children, crowded to the forepart of the vessel. In their maddened despair women jumped overboard; a few minutes more and the mainmast shared the same fate. There yet remained the foremast. As the fire was making its way to the forepart of the vessel, the passengers and crew, of course, crowded still further forward. To the jib boom they clung in clusters as thick as they could pack—even one lying over another. At length the foremast went overboard, snapping the fastenings of the jib boom, which, with its load of human beings, dropped into the water amidst the most heart-rending screams both of those on board and those who were falling into the water. Some of the poor creatures were enabled again to reach the vessel, others floated away on spars, but many met with a watery grave."

In 1849, the *Caleb Grimshaw*, an American packet liner, caught fire. She carried 427 passengers and a thirty-man crew. Crew and passengers fought the fire for several days. The boats finally were lowered but could hold only about 60 people. The remaining steerage passengers continued to struggle with the fire while some of them built a raft and left the ship, never to be seen again. Five days after the fire began a ship arrived and after several stormy nights and days when rescue was impossible, the rescuers managed to take off some passengers. They put a relief crew aboard and sailed the ship to safety in the lee of an island of the Azores group. Altogether 100 people died despite the rescue effort.

Notwithstanding the formidable hazards facing an emigrant to the new world, thousands and thousands of homeless and the poor continued to stream across the Atlantic. And if they survived the merchants of Liverpool, the abusive and sadistic ship's captains and crews, the perils of storm and shipwreck, the ravages of disease, then one fine day the shipload of hopefuls arrived off Sandy Hook where the vessel took aboard a pilot for the final leg of the ocean crossing.

With the opening of the Erie Canal in 1825, and the ascendancy of New York as the major port in America, most immigrants bound for destinations far inland got their first sight of the New World off Sandy Hook. Many Canadian-bound people made their way through the growing city, up the Hudson and then went along a number of different paths to Canada: via the Erie Canal, by lake steamers to the Canadian shore; up the Hudson to Schenectady or Albany and from there along rivers branching off the Hudson northward and eastward, then overland; a few traveled up the New England coast to Nova Scotia. Farmers determined to remove themselves and their families forever from the dominion of the King, headed up the Erie Canal, across the lakes and then by wagon and caravan to the "west" of that day; others filtered north and east into New England looking for the freedom and land for which they had paid such a heavy price.

Yet thousands more, with no great farming instinct but with skills of use in the growing port, remained in New York. Being poor, they soon came across the cruelty and inhumanity of much of the life of that day—which could include a run-in with Gallus Mag or Hell Cat Maggie; or the river gangs of local fame, the Daybreak Boys, Swamp Angels, or the Slaughter Housers. For South Street, in mayhem and murder, was not about to play second fiddle to Liverpool.

When an immigrant ship had passed quarantine and the sick had been removed, the next stop was a pier along South Street. For many it was a rude shock. It is not difficult to picture the surviving, tired, poor immigrant standing with the remains of his luggage and, in many cases, the remaining members of his family. He is, at last, hopeful; he is basking in the glow of that lamp beside the golden door. But no sooner has his ship tied up than the decks are swarming with "runners" from boarding houses and tenements in the port area. Before the immigrant's astonished eyes, the strange scene is changed from one of greeting to, apparently, one of theft. The immigrant's luggage is snatched up, and the snatcher leaps to the dock with it. The immigrant naturally follows, trailed by his weak wife and weaker children. The chase is completed when the immigrant catches up with his retreating worldly goods. And there he is, at a boarding house. And for an exhorbitant price he finds he has a temporary home.

The men who exploited the immigrants were immigrants themselves. They may have arrived a few weeks or months before, but being paupers, they took up any line of work that would keep them alive: even to the skinning of their fellow countrymen.

The immigrants planning to move out of New York City via the Erie Canal were lucky. Those who stayed found lodgings of a permanent nature in such places as Gotham Court—also known as Sweeney's Shambles. It was a long double row of connected tenements at 36 and 38 Cherry Street. Its nickname of Sweeney's Shambles indicates correctly that it frequently was awash with

Hibernian fugitives from the Old Country. The weaker survivors of the ocean voyage quickly sank into complete squalor in such places. If they failed to pay their rents, there was a convenient sewer running beneath Gotham Court for the remains of stubborn, unpaying indigents. The sewer produced a return of its kind in the form of more disease and plague. During one cholera epidemic, the death rate in Sweeney's Shambles reached 195 per thousand people. Of a counted 183 births in the tenement over a three year

Immigrants arriving at South Street often found themselves victimized by fellow countrymen who had preceded them. They also were frequently greeted by sickness and more poverty in the land of the free. *Courtesy Museum of the City of New York.*

period, one out of three infants was dead in less than a month—and a not uncommon cause of death was being bitten to death by huge rats who made the sewer and the walls of the tenement their home.

Exploitation of immigrants became so widespread and efficient that it finally produced two reforming reactions. For once totally broke, the bewildered immigrant became a charge upon the city and state. Eventually the merchants and political leaders saw that the cheap labor of immigrants was being more than offset by poorhouse or "almshouse" and hospital costs. So a commission eventually was set up to handle the flow of immigrants and efforts were directed at moving them on, outside New York, to jobs anywhere they could be located.

The other reaction still has an echo in today's New York. Among poor, hardworking but uncorruptible immigrants who had found a toehold in New York the feeling rose that help should be extended to more lately arriving countrymen. As a first unconscious step toward dispensing this help, immigrants with a common cultural background (ethnic groups, in today's jargon) settled in the same areas. Germans, Irish, Swedes, each stuck together with their own countrymen in a common area. Thus not only were cultural traditions maintained, but their very maintenance provided a defense against the corrupting influences. In time, when Italians and other Mediterranean immigrants arrived, they too established their own "neighborhoods." Soon Societies were formed to welcome and protect immigrants from members' homelands.

So the big, noisy, bawdy hazardous city of New York grew; it absorbed immigrants through the piers along South Street and as each arriving vessel unloaded more of the "wretched refuse" from Europe, many of those immigrants became the solid, middle-class, respected citizens that built America.

6

Today and Tomorrow

OVER A HUNDRED years have passed since South Street was in its heyday. Gone are the *Sea Witch*, and the *Flying Cloud*. Gone too, are Gallus Mag, the Dead Rabbits, the Plug Uglies—and Hell-Cat Maggie resides in some unquiet grave. The packet liners have vanished, the sidewheelers, the tide of immigrants—whose descendants are part of America. The hammers, saws and adzes of the shipyards are quiet and rusting in some forgotten ruin or buried beneath the East River mud. No longer does the air of South Street echo to chanteys of sailors manning capstan bars as ships edge out to meet the tide. The scrimshaw of history is being buried as one by one the gleaming new office buildings rise over the remains of New York's Street of Ships. Apparently progress calls for the obliteration of everything: the good and the bad of yesterday.

Or does it?

On a winter day in 1967, a pedestrian among the remaining buildings of Fulton Street and Schermerhorn Row might have paused in the bitter cold at Number 16 Fulton Street. If it chanced to be late afternoon or early evening along that darkened shambles of a street, he would have noticed lights burning in the dilapidated building. Had he been curious, the pedestrian might have peered through rain-streaked dirty windows and seen two people, a man and a woman, bundled in overcoats, their steaming breath painfully visible on the cold air, busily cleaning and painting the useless interior of the worn-out structure.

Had he passed on with a careless shrug, our pedestrian would never have known that he was witness to the birth of South Street Seaport Museum. Only a crazy man, our now vanished stranger might think, would spend his time in this slum, trying to fix up one tattered building.

And in a sense, the man inside the building—accompanied by his wife—was "crazy." As all people possessed of dreams might be called so. The man was Peter Stanford and his wife, Norma Stanford. The dream was the restoration of South Street; the rebuilding of buildings; the bringing together of historic ships; the dream of making history visible and vital in the world's greatest city of money-grubbers and "practical" men.

Any accountant or economist would have called Peter Stanford mad. Money men do not believe in dreams. Yet what was New York itself to begin with but a dream? Or the United States itself where the money men operate so confidently and successfully

95

Model of the completed South Street Seaport Museum shows the fulfilled dream of preserving this history of New York port. *Photo by Carl T. Scholfield.*

today? Indeed, it is really not money men but dreamers who made the world we know. In any event, Peter Stanford and his wife Norma painted on in the winter nights, warmed only by the dream.

Could a building be purchased? A block of buildings? A whole city block? (In New York City, with those prices to pay? Nonsense.) Two blocks? Maybe more?

Help arrived first in the form of a radiator.

Distressed by their steaming breath, a friend, Richard Rath found and helped to install a radiator so the Stanfords might be warm.

At the outset, so humbly made visible at 16 Fulton Street, Peter Stanford knew that to realize his dream he would have to find a great deal of money. So this man, graduate of Harvard and King's College, Cambridge, yachtsman, publisher and advertising man, began the long uphill climb along the fund-raising trail that ultimately led to success.

Not all practical men have forgotten how to dream. Peter Stanford approached many men of means, talking, persuading, cajoling, creating belief in his dream. The first one to respond and join the dream was Jakob Isbrandsen, shipping executive. Another man of influence, former New York State Senator Whitney North Seymour, obtained passage of a bill in Albany establishing the South Street Maritime Museum Association as a state-sponsored project, with a Board of Trustees appointed by the Governor. His object, initially, was simply to save Schermerhorn Row.

Gradually over the months of 1967, other people joined the ranks of the "dreamers." A "Friends of South Street" group was formed to whom Stanford could appeal for funds, help, furniture, equipment—any critical item for which the need was recognized. He talked to yachtsmen, City Planning people, anyone who would listen. He began a publicity campaign with a carefully prepared flyer, a bimonthly newsletter, and numerous speaking engagements.

By early 1968, the Board of Trustees was functioning and the State of New York gave helpful research time; but also in early 1968, a cloud much bigger than a man's hand loomed over the entire project. Land acquisition for the projected Seaport restoration was coming to a head. Commercial interests and Seaport backers met before the City Planning Commission to seek a decision about the land and the ruins of buildings in the rundown area of South Street. The commercial men wanted the land to put up more gleaming spires as monuments to progress and profit. Peter Stanford, of course, simply wanted his dream to come true.

Not often in the history of such confrontations does the dreamer win. Arguments for practical use of the essentially valuable sites are strong: tax revenue for the hard-pressed city; employment for many workers, during and after construction of more gleaming spires; overall boost to a sagging economy. All these are potent arguments in such battles.

Each side argued. The commercial men spoke of the folly of the dream; they asserted that the old, decrepit buildings were not worth saving. And they touched a nerve among the members of the City Planning Commission. The wrong nerve. For by this time the infectious quality of dreams had spread far beyond Peter and Norma Stanford. Peter Stanford had done his preliminary work well. The dream had caught the imagination of many New Yorkers. The City Planning Commission voted to go on record as favoring the Seaport Museum plan, rather than that of the developers.

Later in 1968, with plans moving forward and hope growing in Seaport backers' hearts, another near calamity struck: real estate speculators bought Schermerhorn Row. They announced plans to put up a large office building there—after tearing down the "old" hulks of buildings. These men, like the commercial men appearing before the Planning Commission, touched the same unsympathetic nerve. Only this time the response was a flood of protests from otherwise cynical New Yorkers. Letters poured into City Hall; the *New York Times* swung its undeniably potent editorial cudgel in defense of the "dream;" a hastily organized "Save South Street" Committee screamed effectively in the halls of City Government. There was, it seems, a real showdown at hand.

The original Planning Commission decision, while important as an advisory statement, was not the critical decision that everyone knew eventually had to be made. The City Board of Estimate is the ruling body on the real decisions. The Board of Estimate met in December of 1968 and Seaport backers pleaded their case. They had, by this time, the backing of a growing and audible number of New York citizens from all income strata. The Board of Estimate listened. Cynical, money-mad New York seemed to have turned into a small village in the naive enthusiasm it showed for South Street Seaport. Inexplicably, history was important; the quality of life in the city—often talked of, rarely realized—was a central issue.

Mayor John Lindsay presided over the hearing. Seaport backers made their plea. The real estate men made theirs. The Seaport won by a vote of 19 to 0. Goose-egged, the real estate men gave up. The dream took another giant step toward realization.

From the beginning, Peter Stanford knew that more than persuasion, more than publicity, had to be the goal. Within the network of down-at-the-heels buildings, along the rotting piers of the East River and between the roaring traffic of trucks and cars, something had to be done visibly; events had to take place. The dream had to become flesh for the unbelieving to see.

In the last months of 1967, Stanford sent out invitations to all the countries of the world that still used sailing ships to train their naval and merchant marine cadets. He offered the Seaport Pier as docking space should any of the great sailing ships left on the seas come to New York. The U. S. Coast Guard training ship *Eagle* responded, as did Denmark's square-rigger, *Danmark*.

The Coast Guard training ship *Eagle* was one of the first working ships to visit South Street. *Courtesy South Street Seaport Museum.*

In the spring of 1968, to mark the anniversary of the side-wheel steamer *Savannah* on her first steam-powered transatlantic voyage in 1819, a brief festive cruise aboard the operating *Alexander Hamilton*, a side-wheeler of ancient years, was held. Guests paid for a dinner and ball aboard the ship as she moved sedately down the Hudson to the Statue of Liberty and returned.

Negotiations were completed in 1968 for the purchase of the

museum's first major ship acquisition, the steel-hulled sailing ship *Wavertree*. Publicity surrounding the purchase—with pictures of the ship's battered hull in Buenos Aires, Argentina, kept the idea of the museum alive in the minds of New Yorkers.

As early as 1967, the idea of an annual schooner race took hold. Sponsored by the then fledgling Museum, it drew a sizeable number of these heartwarming traditionally rigged ships to New York Harbor, a gala dinner in the evening following the race drew the newly christened Mayor's Cup as prize to the winner.

The race was repeated in 1968. More schooners joined the race and the waters of New York Bay were covered that October day by more sail than New Yorkers had seen since the beginning of the twentieth century. Television coverage, special excursion steamers crowded with observers, newspaper reporters and a host of shore-bound well-wishers focused attention on the new embodied dream of South Street Museum.

Undoubtedly the most surprised people were captains and crews of incoming ships. They arrived at the Narrows and gazed up the Bay to see, not twentieth century New York boats plying the waters, but filled sails of schooners tacking across their bows. A surprised captain of a large cargo ship might well have rubbed his eyes and wondered if time had not been rolled back. Indeed, for the briefest moment it had.

To interest the average citizen, Stanford organized early a series of summer walking tours through the debris littered streets where volunteers pointed out buildings and sites that would some day be what they were over a hundred years ago. And looking at those streets then it would have seemed a discouraging dream. In some godforsaken empty lot covered with refuse and dead fish smelling as only dead fish can smell, a smiling, enthusiastic volunteer would exclaim over the building that would rise there. Before a sad crumpled looking storefront at another point, still another smiling volunteer would exclaim over the trim elegant look that building would have when once it was put back together.

But the people came, by the thousands, and left infected if only to a small degree by the dream.

Knowing he had to catch the hearts and minds of even the sceptical, Peter Stanford authorized the expenditure of $30,000 to construct a realistic model of the completed dream: Five and a half blocks of valuable New York City real estate to contain 68 restored buildings; four piers to berth the ships; the place alive with gift shops, restaurants, handcraft shops; food markets; taverns—all the activities that marked the Seaport in its heyday. And these were planned not to be still-life replicas, but actual working establishments, the spaces leased, the income to support the museum. A theatre, an educational center, several shipping museums: a genuine port of call. Tours, cruises aboard the refurbished historic ships, tours of visiting ships from other lands—all these would combine to make the South Street project a living, breathing dream. A dream that began in the winter of 1967, in the cold air, in the dirt and debris of a hopeless old wreck of a building at 16 Fulton Street.

The First Ships

They almost got away. The ships. Old hulls rotting at wharves all over the world: Maine, The Falkland Islands, Valparaiso, Portsmouth. They rotted and sank into the mud. No one cared. Their day was over.

Yet they had settled the world we know today. By 1850, all new lands had been discovered; the first settlers had arrived. All the great and hazardous sea routes had been charted, and sailed.

The vessels that had accomplished this were thrown away. The men who sailed them had died. Here and there a few ships were saved, historic by virtues of a voyage or merely longevity: The *Charles W. Morgan*, the *Cutty Sark*, *Old Ironsides*, *H.M.S. Discovery*. The rest were beached in forgotten coves or turned into lowly barges hauling coal or garbage or grain in estuaries and bays —masts gone, nothing left but the indestructibly beautiful lines of the hull. But what a fate! No one who saw the beached hulls or the great hulls being towed as barges could suppress a spasm of pain.

South Street Seaport has saved a few. In the original dream of the restored Seaport, Peter Stanford knew that ships would play an important part. He knew they would cost a fortune to find, refurbish and bring to New York. He also knew that if he and his colleagues didn't do it, no one would.

But the dream went further than the simple restoration and display of old ships. The dream included living ships, capable of slipping their lines on a bright day and going down river to catch the tide and go once more again to sea.

In the earliest days of the Seaport's life, plans to restore Schermerhorn Row had to be delayed. Sensing that something real had to be accomplished, the Seaport Directors focused their attention on acquiring, repairing, and bringing to South Street's piers one of the last square riggers on the globe.

The Wavertree

She is 279 feet long, steel-hulled, with a beam of 40.2 feet and she first touched water in Southampton, England in 1885. The *Wavertree* is a full-rigged ship, built to the order of R. W. Leyland & Brothers of Liverpool by Oswalk Mordaunt & Company.

Sold, sailed and repurchased by Leyland & Brothers, the *Wavertree* entered the last days of sail doing what full-rigged ships of the later nineteenth century had to do: Tramp for cargo all over the globe.

Steam had taken the good cargoes. First ports of the world saw fewer and fewer of the tall masted sailing ships. But out of the way places became the *Wavertree*'s ports of call. She sailed for India and Australia across the Indian Ocean and round the Cape of Good Hope. Her cargoes were grain or jute—cargoes of high volume and low price.

From Sydney, Australia one fine day in 1891, she set sail for San

The *Wavertree* as she appeared at the turn of the century leaving New York port. She was acquired by the museum in 1968. *Courtesy South Street Seaport Museum.*

105

Francisco across the Pacific, then down around Cape Horn, that nemesis of ships. Her first passage of these waters of mountainous seas and hurricane winds was "the easy way" from west to east, off the wind and moving fast.

By rights a ship the size of the *Wavertree* ought to have been a four-masted bark. Such a rig would have reduced the size of single sails, made her easier to tack and saved the breath of many a sailor aloft as he hauled on canvas too big for easy grasp. But she was three-masted full-rigged, hard to tack, and a devil to change sail on. Her three wooden masts supported mammoth hollow iron yards. The huge sails were oversized and did not admit of quick handling.

In 1892 she sailed into New York for the first time. Then down to Rio, around the Horn to the nitrate ports of Chile. The east to west passage of Cape Horn is the worst way, the hard way. Prevailing winds sweep this dismal stretch of sea blowing dead against a ship's course. Storms are the usual, good weather the abnormal. Ice, sleet, icebergs, hurricane force winds all add to the hazards that have made Cape Horn the legend of destruction that it is.

The *Wavertree* made the passage many times. And it was on such a voyage, westbound through Drake's Passage, 200 miles south of the Cape in August, 1910, that disaster set in. August, by the way, in those latitudes, corresponds to the season we ordinarily experience in February in the northern hemisphere. Seas rolled unobstructed, forever under the howling wind. Doubtless ice, snow, and sleet hammered the vessel and her yards must have been coated in ice. The gale ripped away most of *Wavertree*'s huge sails and she turned back to Montevideo, rigged new canvas and set out again, driving south, then west around Cape Horn.

Later that same year, in December, the end came for *Wavertree*. Another Cape gale dismasted her. She lost her mainmast plus her fore and mizzen topmasts. Unmanageable, she drifted east with the winds and currents, a helpless wreck. Two of her boats had been smashed and seawater had fouled all the drinking water aboard. When the gale blew out, she was sighted and taken in tow for the Falkland Islands, coming ignominiously into port at Stanley the day before Christmas.

Wavertree lay in Stanley for months. Her owners decided she was not worth the expense of re-fitting. She was towed to Punta Arenas and there served as a floating warehouse—all hint of her proud sailing days over save for the ineradicable lines of her hull. Thirty-seven years passed. Then she was towed to Buenos Aires to be scrapped. But her staunch hull still had some useful days and she was converted to a sand dredge. In this menial capacity the ship "lived" for twenty more years.

Rescue came at last to *Wavertree*. In 1968, South Street Seaport gained possession of her, the task of repairing her hull to meet the seas once more was undertaken and in August, 1970, she came through the Narrows and entered New York harbor. It has been her home port ever since.

Lettie G. Howard

Say ketch. Say yawl. Say sloop. Now try, schooner. Say gaff-rigged schooner. And now you really have an audience.

No other ship's rig, save perhaps a square-rigged ship, draws as much attention as a Gloucester fishing schooner, or a fair approximation of one.

For some time one of the South Street Seaport's two schooners was believed to be the rebuilt *Caviare* whose keel was laid down in 1891. Later research disclosed that in all probability the schooner was the rebuilt *Lettie G. Howard* also of Gloucester fishing fame. The confusion is understandable. Many schooners of that era had reached a point of hull design perfection, and rigging that made

The *Lettie G. Howard*, a South Street ship, sailed first for cod off the Grand Banks, later for red snapper in the Gulf of Mexico. *Courtesy South Street Seaport Museum.*

them fast, serviceable fishing boats for the northern cod fisheries. The gaff-rigged fishing boats raced, fished, weathered storms and generally dominated the waters from Massachusetts north. Indeed the profile of one could easily have served as an emblem of New England in those days.

Soon after the turn of the century, southern fishermen in the Gulf of Mexico discovered the serviceability of these stout craft—so large combines bought the schooners secondhand, had them sailed to the Gulf and instead of catching cod, they caught red snappers.

Such was the fate of many schooners, among them *Lettie G. Howard*, *Caviare*, and another famous schooner now lost, *Lottie S. Haskins*—a sister ship of *Caviare*.

One by one the aging schooners began to "die" in the warm southern waters where temperatures, salinity and marine worms all combined to attack hulls and the fastenings. Many were surveyed and abandoned: the *Caviare* in 1916, *Lottie S. Haskins* in 1920, and *Lettie G. Howard* in March of 1923.

In May of that year, a rebuilt schooner renamed *Mystic C.* took to the waters and sailed for more red snappers until the mid-sixties. Believing the schooner to be the *Caviare*, the Seaport acquired ownership and brought what its Directors believed was the *Caviare*, north for another refurbishing. For two years the schooner called *Caviare* lived again. She sailed on summer cruises up the Sound, to Martha's Vineyard, Nantucket, Cape Cod, taking on each cruise young lubbers from New York City and turning them into sailors.

In 1971, evidence turned up that the schooner was indeed the *Lettie G. Howard*. For the *Caviare* was abandoned in 1916 and it would have been nearly impossible to rebuild her after seven years of inattention in tropic waters. Records of a marine railway that hauled boats for the owners of the schooner fleet show that the

Lettie G. Howard was hauled in March, 1923. In May, a schooner was put into the water and in the record book the words *Lettie G. Howard* were crossed out and *Mystic C.* pencilled in. So strong was the evidence, the Ship Committee of the Seaport renamed the schooner, giving back her true maiden name.

Ambrose Lightship

In the great age of shipping, millions of passengers first knew they were on New York's doorstep when the plump hull of the *Ambrose Lightship* was sighted. For an equal number of people, she was the last view of the United States as their ships steamed out into the Atlantic, bound for Europe or other distant lands. "The landfall or departure for millions of hopes and memories," as one newspaper put it.

No port in the United States, large or small, operates without a multitude of "Aids to Navigation." Lighthouses, beacons, radar stations, buoys, bells, whistles; they are many and varied. And in the first half of the twentieth century, lightships, firmly anchored in one spot and manned by patient, isolated crews, served their time and became a part of the legend of the sea. *Ambrose Lightship* is part of the legend of New York port.

Built in Camden, New Jersey in 1907, *Ambrose* is steelhulled, steam powered (with a schooner sail rig) and was manned by five officers and ten men. She was in place at the seaward end of the then newly dredged Ambrose Channel designed to provide a safe route for the largest ships afloat into and out of the formerly unstable entrance to the harbor of New York.

Altogether, ten lightships similar to *Ambrose* were built at the same time and for decades their squat hulls, bobbing ceaselessly on the sea were familiar sights to all aboard vessels sailing to Europe. On their sides were painted their stations, in large letters for immediate visual identification in good daylight weather. At night, strong beacons flashed intermittently from their specially constructed masts. In fog and low visibility, horns and bells sent regulated bursts of sound across the waters to warn and assist incoming and outgoing ships. They had the isolation of the lighthouse but did not share the safety of those shorebound beacons high above storm waves.

The *Ambrose*, a lightship retired by the Coast Guard in 1965. She once guided ships in and out of the harbor. *Courtesy South Street Seaport Museum.*

111

Among officers and crew aboard the lightships, fear of being rammed while helplessly at anchor was part of the assignment. And it had happened to other lightships in the past. The *Nantucket Shoals Lightship* had been run down by a steamer. The *Fire Island Lightship* had been hit by a steamer, the *Castilian*. And another lightship, temporarily anchored on Ambrose station had been rammed during a thick fog.

Ambrose Lightship remained on her station for more than twenty years, her only contact with the "outside" world being the weekly supply ship that serviced her from Staten Island. Occasionally, fishing boats would come alongside and toss magazines and newspapers aboard but by and large crew members could only gaze at the surrounding bustle of ship traffic and the more distant life of the landsmen.

In 1936, in an unusual flurry of activity, *Ambrose Lightship* was assigned to Scotland station, off Sandy Hook, New Jersey. The word AMBROSE was painted out and SCOTLAND painted in. This station was originally established over the wreck of the British steamer, *Scotland* to mark the spot and prevent other ships from being wrecked on the steamer's remains. And after the wreck itself was removed, a lightship stayed as a permanent aid to navigation in the approaches to New York harbor.

World War II was a period of rest for all lightships. They were removed to prevent enemy ships or submarines from using them to identify their positions. Fear of hit-and-run raids on the coast, or the landing of spies was great then and the additional hazard to our own ships in navigating the shoals and channels of the harbor entrance unassisted was considered worth taking.

The entrance to New York harbor has been marked by a light or lights visible from the sea since 1764. In that year, Sandy Hook lighthouse was built and went into service. During the Revolution attempts were made to extinguish the comforting light signal by

British troops. When the British controlled the area around Sandy Hook, Continental troops in their turn raided the light to put it out. No success came to either side.

The first lightship went into service in 1823 and she was a wooden vessel named *Sandy Hook*. All through the great growth period of South Street, through the Civil War and afterward, wooden lightships marked the harbor entrance.

At the turn of the century, ships were becoming larger, drawing more water and frequently having difficulty with the silting shifting bottom of the entrance to the harbor. A Government engineer named John W. Ambrose fought for nearly two decades to have the Government dredge a deep permanent channel that would serve the world's shipping. Whether the deciding factor was engineer Ambrose's pleading or the increase in ship's size, the Government appropriated money in 1899 and the channel was dug. It is 2000 feet wide, six miles long and provides a forty-foot depth at low tide. Marked by buoys along its side, and the early *Ambrose Lightship* in 1908, the channel was named Ambrose in honor of its advocate.

In 1939, the old Light House Service that had charge of ship and land-based lights was taken over by the Coast Guard and *Ambrose Lightship* became WAL-512. Following World War II, she was assigned duty in Vineyard Sound, a well-traveled body of water lying between the south shore of Cape Cod and the island of Martha's Vineyard. Two years later, she returned to familiar waters: Scotland station off Sandy Hook.

Progress began to overtake the aging lightship. Development of fixed beacon and radar towers as navigational aids brought an end to *Ambrose*'s usefulness in 1964. After a brief tour at the New York World's Fair in 1965, the Ambrose was decommissioned and stored in Curtis Bay, Baltimore.

Today, as a member of South Street's fleet of historic vessels,

Ambrose serves as a small museum of Coast Guard activities over the years. No port and no ocean-going ship can function without the help of the navigational aids provided by this Government Service. The lives of all men of the sea and occasional passengers on the water are protected, and have been protected, by such historic vessels WAL-512, *Ambrose Lightship*.